101 WAYS TO IMPROVE YOUR *Vocabulary*

101 WAYS TO IMPROVE YOUR *Vocabulary*

ROBERT WHITE
Department of English
Jamestown High School
Jamestown, New York

A NAUTILUS COMMUNICATIONS BOOK

ARCO PUBLISHING, INC.

Crossword Puzzles courtesy of Superb Crossword Puzzle Magazine, Official Publications, Inc., New York City

Published by Arco Publishing, Inc.
215 Park Avenue South, New York, N.Y. 10003

Copyright © 1983 by Nautilus Communications, Inc.

All rights reserved. No part of this book may be reproduced, by any means, without permission in writing from the publisher, except by a reviewer who wishes to quote brief excerpts in connection with a review in a magazine or newspaper.

Library of Congress Cataloging in Publication Data

White, Robert, 1948–
  101 ways to improve your vocabulary.

  "A Nautilus communications book."
  1. Vocabulary. I. Title. II. Title: One hundred one ways to improve your vocabulary. III. Title: One Hundred and one ways to improve your vocabulary.
PE1449.W42   1983   428.1   83-12243
ISBN 0-668-05658-4 (pbk.)

Printed in the United States of America

CONTENTS

INTRODUCTION 1
PREFIX AND SUFFIX LIST 4
ROOTS 11
PUZZLES 159
ANSWERS 163

INTRODUCTION

If you want to improve and increase your vocabulary, this book is for you. It is not a typical book of vocabulary words. Instead, the focus is on developing the ability to understand words and their patterns, and to recognize the *roots* of the words.

Every word in the English language has a basic meaning. A word normally begins with a root, which may be the complete word, or may be part of the whole word. To this root you may add a *prefix* (a word-part that appears in front of a root to change the meaning) or a *suffix* (a word-part that appears at the end of a root).

For example, let's look at a typical root: *DUC* or *DUCT*. This root means *lead*. If we add a prefix to the root, we can change the meaning. The prefix *con* means *together*. Now we have the word *con-duct*—to lead together.

Very simple, isn't it? Now let's add a suffix. The suffix *ion* means *process* or *act of*. If we combine the root with a prefix and a suffix, here's what we have:

        Prefix—in (means *in*)
        Root—duc (means *lead*)
        Suffix—tion (means *act of*)

We now have *in-duc-tion*, the *act of leading into*. To lead someone into the army is called an *induction*.

This root can also stand on its own. A *duct* is usually a pipe or tube to lead something through. For example, a tear duct is the channel through which tears can flow. A water duct is a pipe through which water will flow.

Try another one. The root *CRED* means, *to believe*. If we add the prefix *in* (which also means *not* as well as *in*), and the suffix *ible* (which means *able to*) we have:

        Prefix—in (means *not*)
        Root—cred (means *to believe*)
        Suffix—ible (means *able to*)

We now have *in-cred-ible*, which means *not able to be believed*.

By using roots as the core to your vocabulary, and then adding different prefixes and suffixes, you will develop an enormous flexibility with words. It will help your vocabulary grow and will give you confidence in your ability to use words creatively.

How To Use This Book

We have developed this book on a daily lesson plan to help you develop your vocabulary easily and painlessly. Each root is a complete lesson. You will see the root, and it will be defined. Try to learn that root before going on to the next lesson. Every lesson has several words defined for you. This is to help you recognize the root in actual use.

Following the examples are a few words that will require you to find the definition. Try to develop the word yourself. If you can't, look it up in the dictionary, or turn to the answers in the back of the book. Once you look up the word, it will stay with you.

The last section of each lesson is usually another type of exercise, including matching words and synonyms, or more definitions. Using what you've learned about the root, do your best to help develop the words and understand the correct answers.

There is also a section at the beginning of the book which includes prefixes and suffixes. Read through the lists and use them to create words. Use that section as a reference when you try to deduce word definitions.

One very good way to practice what you have learned, as well as continuing to increase your vocabulary, is to do the daily crossword puzzles in your local newspapers. Not only are they fun, but they definitely help increase your collection of words. Don't be afraid to look up words in a crossword puzzle dictionary. We have included a few

Introduction

crossword puzzles to test your ability to locate and define words. Again, do your best, and then check the answers.

Work on these lessons diligently. If you don't understand a lesson, repeat it until it becomes comprehensible. If you do one lesson daily, you will quickly develop a vocabulary that will impress everyone—especially yourself. Good luck!

PREFIX AND SUFFIX LIST

Prefixes

Prefix	Meaning	Examples
a-	in, on, of, to	abed—in bed
a-, ab-, abs-	from, away	abrade—wear off absent—away, not present
a-, an-	lacking, not	asymptomatic—showing no symptoms anaerobic—able to live without air
ad-, ac-, af-, ag-, al-, an-, ap-, ar-, as-, at-	to, toward	accost—approach and speak to adjunct—something added to aggregate—bring together
ambi, amphi-	around, both	ambidextrous—using both hands equally amphibious—living both in water and on land
ana-	up, again, anew, throughout	analyze—loosen up, break up into parts anagram—word spelled by mixing up letters of another word
ante-	before	antediluvian—before the Flood
anti-	against	antiwar—against war
arch-	first, chief	archetype—first model

Prefix and Suffix List

auto-	self	automobile—self-moving vehicle
bene-, ben-	good, well	benefactor—one who does good deeds
bi-	two	bilateral—two-sided
circum-	around	circumnavigate—sail around
com-, co-, col-, con-, cor-	with, together	concentrate—bring closer together
		cooperate—work with
		collapse—fall together
contra-, contro-, counter-	against	contradict—speak against
		counterclockwise—against the clock
de-	away from, down, opposite of	detract—draw away from
demi-	half	demitasse—half cup
di-	twice, double	dichromatic—having two colors
dia-	across, through	diameter—measurement across
dis-, di	not, away from	dislike—to not like
		digress—turn away from the subject
dys-	bad, poor	dyslexia—poor reading
equi-	equal	equivalent—of equal value
ex-, e-, ef-	from, out	expatriate—one who lives outside his native country
		emit—send out
extra-	outside, beyond	extraterrestrial—from beyond the earth
fore-	in front of, previous	forecast—tell ahead of time
		foreleg—front leg
geo-	earth	geography—science of the earth's surface

homo-	same, like	homophonic—sounding the same
hyper-	too much, over	hyperactive—overly active
hypo-	too little, under	hypothermia—state of having too little body heat
in-, il-, ig-, im-, ir-	not	innocent—not guilty ignorant—not knowing illogical—not logical irresponsible—not responsible
in-, il-, im-, ir-,	on, into, in	impose—place on invade—go into
inter-	between, among	interplanetary—between planets
intra-, intro-,	within, inside	intrastate—within a state
mal-, male-	bad, wrong, poor	maladjust—adjust poorly malevolent—ill-wishing
mis-	badly, wrongly	misunderstand—understand wrongly
mis-, miso-	hatred	misogyny—hatred of women
mono-	single, one	monorail—train that runs on a single rail
neo-	new	neolithic—of the New Stone Age
non-	not	nonentity—a nobody
ob-	over, against, toward	obstruct—stand against
omni-	all	omnipresent—present in all places
pan-	all	panorama—a complete view
peri-	around, near	periscope—device for seeing all around
poly-	many	polygonal—many-sided
post-	after	postmortem—after death

Prefix and Suffix List

Prefix	Meaning	Examples
pre-	before, earlier than	prejudice—judgment in advance
pro-	in favor of, forward, in front of	proceed—go forward prowar—in favor of war
re-	back, again	rethink—think again reimburse—pay back
retro-	backward	retrospective—looking backward
se-	apart, away	seclude—keep away
semi-	half	semiconscious—half conscious
sub-, suc-, suf-, sug-, sus-	under, beneath	subscribe—write underneath suspend—hang down suffer—undergo
super-	above, greater	superfluous—overflowing, beyond what is needed
syn-, sym-, syl-, sys-	with, at the same time	synthesis—a putting together sympathy—a feeling with
tele-	far	television—machine for seeing far
trans-	across	transport—carry across a distance
ult-	beyond, last	ultramarine—beyond the sea
un-	not	uninformed—not informed
vice-	acting for, next in rank to	viceroy—one acting for the king

Suffixes

Suffix	*Meaning*	*Examples*
-able, -ble,	able, capable	acceptable—able to be accepted

-acious, -cious	characterized by, having the quality of	fallacious—having the quality of a fallacy
-age	sum, total	mileage—total number of miles
-al	of, like, suitable for	theatrical—suitable for theater
-ance, -ancy	act or state of	disturbance—act of disturbing
-ant, -ent	one who	defendant—one who defends himself
-ary, -ar	having the nature of, concerning	military—relating to soldiers polar—concerning the pole
-cise, -cide	cut, kill	herbacide—plant killer
-cy	act, state, or position of	presidency—position of president ascendency—state of being raised up
-dom	state, rank, that which belongs to	wisdom—state of being wise
-ence	act, state, or quality of	dependence—state of depending
-er, -or	one who, that which	doer—one who does conductor—that which conducts
-escent	becoming	obsolescent—becoming obsolete
-fy	to make	pacify—make peaceful
-hood	state, condition	adulthood—state of being adult
-ic, -ac	of, like	demonic—of or like a demon
-il, -ile	having to do with, like, suitable for	civil—having to do with citizens tactile—having to do with touch
-ion	act or condition of	operation—act of operating
-ious	having, characterized by	anxious—characterized by anxiety
-ish	like, somewhat	foolish—like a fool

Prefix and Suffix List

-ism	belief or practice of	racism—belief in racial superiority
-ist	one who does, makes or is concerned with	scientist—one concerned with science
-ity, -ty, -y	character or state of being	amity—friendship jealousy—state of being jealous
-ive	of, relating to, tending to	destructive—tending to destroy
-logue, -loquy	speech or writing	monologue—speech by one person colloquy—conversation
-logy	speech, study of	geology—study of the earth
-ment	act or state of	abandonment—act of abandoning
-mony	a resulting thing, condition, or state	patrimony—property inherited from one's father
-ness	act or quality	kindness—quality of being kind
-ory	having the quality of; a place or thing for	compensatory—having the quality of a compensation lavatory—place for washing
-ous, -ose	full of, having	glamorous—full of glamor
-ship	skill, state of being	horsemanship—skill in riding ownership—state of being an owner
-some	full of, like	frolicsome—playful
-tude	state or quality of	rectitude—state of being morally upright
-ward	in the direction of	homeward—in the direction of home
-y	full of, like, somewhat	wily—full of wiles

ROOTS

Lesson 1

ROOT: ACER, ACID, ACRI
MEANING: bitter, sour, sharp

Example
acerb
acid
acrimonious

Meaning
bitter to the taste, sharp
a sharp, burning or bitter substance
nagging, bitterness

Test Yourself

Define the following words.

1. acerate _____
2. acidemia _____
3. acerbate _____
4. acidulate _____
5. acidic _____

Recognizing Words

In the following questions, select the word that is *closest* in meaning to the key word.

6. acidity
   a. closeness   b. foul odor
   c. sourness   d. vulgar
7. acidosis
   a. speed trap   b. blood disease
   c. sharp noise   d. angered
8. acute
   a. perceptive   b. angled
   c. negative   d. pleased
9. acerbic
   a. tyrannical   b. sharp wit
   c. tired   d. pliant

(Answers on page 163.)

Lesson 2

ROOT: AG, AGI, AGO
MEANING: to move, do, drive

Example | Meaning
agent — person representing another
agile — able to move quickly, active
agog — eager
agitant — one who is active

Test Yourself

Define the following words.

1. agency _____
2. agenda _____
3. antagonist _____

Recognizing Words

Fill in the blank with the proper word.

4. The football player moved with surprising _____. (ability to move quickly)

5. Her brother continued to _____ her. (annoy)

6. The frenzied audience _____ the usually calm performer. (disturbed)

7. The decision was difficult, and he _____ over it. (suffered)

8. The land baron _____ his holdings by ruthlessly evicting the tenant farmers. (made greater)

(Answers on page 163.)

Lesson 3

ROOT: AL, ALL, ALTER
MEANING: other

Example | Meaning
alias — an assumed name
altruist — a person unselfishly concerned with other people's welfare
alter — to change slightly
altercation — a fight or dispute

Test Yourself
Define the following words.

1. alibi _____
2. allegory _____
3. inalienable _____
4. alienate _____
5. allogamy _____

Recognizing Words

In the following questions, select the word that is *closest* in meaning to the key word.

6. alienable
   a. fixed   b. transferable
   c. torpid   d. tired
7. alteration
   a. difficulty   b. choice
   c. unusual   d. change
8. alternate
   a. use sparingly b. speak slowly
   c. take turns   d. move cautiously
9. allotypical
   a. other types   b. green plant
   c. unfairly   d. temperate

(Answers on page 163.)

Lesson 4

ROOT: ANN, ENN
MEANING: year

Example
per annum
biennial
centennial
annuity

Meaning
(Latin) for a year
once every two years
once every hundred years
a sum of money paid every year

Test Yourself
Define the following words.

1. anniversary _____
2. triennial   _____
3. bicentennial _____
4. annualize   _____

Recognizing Words

Match the appropriate words in each column.

5. decennial   a. yearly
6. tricentennial   b. every hundred years
7. millennial   c. every eight years
8. centennial   d. every ten years
9. octennial   e. every three-hundred years
10. annual   f. every thousand years

(Answers on page 163.)

Lesson 5

ROOT: **ANTHROP**
MEANING: man, human being

Example
anthropoid
anthropic
misanthropy
anthropophagy
anthroponomy

Meaning
resembling man
pertaining to mankind
hatred of mankind
cannibalism
the science of human behavior

Test Yourself

Define the following words.

1. philanthropy _____
2. anthropomorphism _____
3. anthropocentric _____
4. anthropogenesis _____
5. anthropometer _____
6. anthropology _____
7. anthropography _____
8. anthropologist _____

(Answers on page 164.)

Lesson 6

ROOT: ARCH
MEANING: ruler, leader, first

Example	Meaning
anarchy	a rulerless state
archenemy	a principal opponent
archangel	a chief angel
tetrarchy	a government of four people
genarch	head of a family

Test Yourself

Define the following words.

1. hierarch _____
2. archbishop _____
3. architect _____
4. archetype _____
5. panarchy _____

Recognizing Words

Match the word with the correct definition.

6. monarchy
7. matriarch
8. patriarch
9. oligarchy
10. pentarchy

a. female head of tribe or family
b. government by the few
c. government ruled by five leaders
d. a single ruler
e. male head of tribe or family

(Answers on page 164.)

Lesson 7

ROOT: ASTER, ASTR
MEANING: star

Example
astronomy

astrometer

astrograph

Meaning
science and study of heavenly bodies
device used to measure heavenly bodies
a photo/telescope

Test Yourself

Define the following words.

1. astrology _____
2. astrolabe _____
3. astrography _____
4. astronomer _____
5. asteroid _____

Recognizing Words

For each of the definitions below, provide a word that best defines the word.

6. Combined study of astronomy and physics to understand the heavens. _____

7. A space traveller. _____

8. A star-shaped cell. _____

9. The starlike character used in printing and writing. _____

(Answers on page 164.)

Lesson 8

ROOT: AUDI
MEANING: to hear, listen

Example
audible
audience
audivision

Meaning
easily heard
a group of listeners
sound accompanying pictures

Test Yourself
Define the following words.

1. auditorium _____
2. audio _____
3. audience _____
4. audiotape _____
5. audiovisual _____

Recognizing Words

Select the appropriate word.

6. The sound was _____, so he turned it up. (hard to hear)

7. Her accountant insisted upon the _____. (a formal examination of the books)

8. They rehearsed continuously for their _____. (a hearing by judge of talent)

9. His deafness was caused by damage to the _____ nerves. (related to hearing ability)

10. The musician was a devoted _____. (One who loves high quality sound reproduction)

(Answers on page 164.)

Lesson 9

ROOT: BIO
MEANING: life

Example
biology
biota
biographer

biostatics
bionics

Meaning
the study of living things
plant and animal life of a region
person who writes about another's life
structure of organisms
study of the relationship between man and machine

Test Yourself

Define the following words.

1. biologist _____
2. biography _____
3. biopsy _____
4. biogenesis _____
5. autobiography _____
6. biome _____
7. bioplasm _____
8. bioclimatic _____
9. biomedicine _____
10. biosphere _____

(Answers on page 165.)

Lesson 10

ROOT: CAL, CALOR
MEANING: heat, hot

Example
calorie
scald
calenture

Meaning
a unit of heat
to burn with hot water
tropical fever caused by exposure to heat

Test Yourself

Define the following words.

1. caloric
2. calorific
3. calorimeter
4. calorimetry
5. calorize
6. caldron

(Answers on page 165.)

Lesson 11

ROOT: CAP, CEP, CEPT
MEANING: take, receive

Example
capable
capacity
conception
captor

Meaning
able to receive learning
able to receive or contain
act of conceiving
one who takes by force

Test Yourself

Define the following words.

1. capacitor   _____
2. perceptive   _____
3. susceptible   _____
4. accept   _____
5. deception   _____

Recognizing Words

In the following examples, select the word that is *closest* in meaning to the key word.

6. intercept   a. seize   b. pass
                   c. throw   d. change
7. captivate   a. dance   b. charm
                   c. attempt   d. interfere
8. receptacle   a. glasses   b. container
                   c. whole   d. passive
9. capsule   a. height   b. container
                   c. bullet   d. flier

(Answers on page 165.)

Lesson 12

ROOT: CAPIT, CAPT
MEANING: leader, chief, head

Example
captain
caption
capital
capitalism

capitulum

Meaning
an officer
a heading
chief in importance
economic system believing in free enterprise
a flower head

Test Yourself

Define the following words.

1. capitulate _____
2. per capita _____
3. capitular _____
4. capital gain _____
5. capo _____

Recognizing Words

Match the appropriate words in each column.

6. capitalize
7. decapitate
8. recapitulate
9. capitol
10. capitation

a. repeat or restate
b. seat of government
c. lose one's head
d. tax on one's head (poll tax)
e. make a profit

(Answers on page 165.)

Lesson 13

ROOT: CARD, COR, CORD, COUR
MEANING: heart

Example
core
courage
courageous
record
cardiac

Meaning
the center, the heart
bravery
to have heart, brave
preserve information
pertaining to the heart

Test Yourself

Define the following words.

1. cordial _____
2. encouraged _____
3. accord _____
4. discord _____
5. cardiogram _____
6. concord _____
7. cordate _____

(Answers on page 166.)

Lesson 14

ROOT: CAUSE, CUS, CUSE
MEANING: motive

Example
cause
because
inexcusable
accuser

causal

Meaning
reason, motive
for that reason
can be forgiven
a person who charges another with crime
implying a motive

Test Yourself

Define the following words.

1. accuse _____
2. excuse (v) _____
3. excuse (n) _____
4. causeless _____
5. causality _____
6. causationism _____

(Answers on page 166.)

Lesson 15

ROOT: CEDE, CEED, CESS
MEANING: yield, surrender, to go

Example
cede
ancestor
recession
secede

Meaning
to admit, yield
relative from whom one is descended
a going back
to separate, to pull away from

Test Yourself
Define the following words.

1. intercede
2. precedent
3. decease
4. exceed
5. process

Recognizing Words

In the following examples, select the word that is *closest* in meaning to the key word.

6. accede   a. priority   b. agree to
             c. falter   d. talk
7. concede   a. force   b. play for
             c. yield to   d. dissuade
8. succeed   a. imply   b. dissolve
             c. achieve   d. prior
9. recede   a. sail   b. drift
             c. hover   d. withdraw
10. incessant   a. weepy   b. careful
             c. continuing   d. without

(Answers on page 166.)

Lesson 16

ROOT: CHROM, CHRO
MEANING: color

Example
chrom
chromatometer

chromatin

chromogenic
monochrome

Meaning
a color pigment
device for measuring perception of colors
stainable substance of cell nucleus
producing colors
painting with several shades of one color

Test Yourself

Define the following words.

1. chromatic _____
2. chromoplast _____
3. chromophil _____
4. panchromatic _____
5. monochromatic _____
6. monochromatism _____
7. dichromic _____

(Answers on page 166.)

Lesson 17

ROOT: CHRON
MEANING: time

Example
chronic
chronometer
chronologer
synchronize

Meaning
continuing a long time
instrument for measuring time
expert in the science of measuring time
to happen at the same time

Test Yourself

Define the following words.

1. chronology   _____
2. synchroscope _____
3. chronopher   _____
4. chronicler   _____
5. chronoscope   _____

Recognizing Words

Match the words to their corresponding definitions.

6. chronograph
7. chronicle
8. synchronism
9. chronography
10. chronothermal

a. a record of events
b. the state of existing at the same time
c. involving time and temperature
d. device to measure time intervals
e. historical record in order of time

(Answers on page 166.)

Lesson 18

ROOT: CIV
MEANING: citizen

Example	Meaning
civic	relating to a citizen
civilization	man's cultural development
civil defense	plans for protection of civilians and property
civil service	government service other than military
civism	principles of citizenship

Recognizing Words

Select the appropriate word.

1. Once he left the army, he was a _____. (not a soldier)

2. They taught their children to act with _____. (politeness)

3. The teenagers were _____ to the adults. (rude)

4. The war between North and South Vietnam began as a _____. (battle between political factions within the same country)

5. The settlers tried to _____ the Indians. (to enlighten, bring out of barbarism)

(Answers on page 167.)

Lesson 19

ROOT: CLAIM, CLAM
MEANING: to declare, call out, cry out

Example
claim
proclamation
clamorous
reclaim
irreclaimable

Meaning
to call one's own
a public notice
full of noise
to attempt to regain
cannot be reclaimed

Test Yourself

Define the following words.

1. declaim _____
2. disclaim _____
3. exclamation _____
4. unclaimed _____
5. claimant _____
6. claim jumper _____
7. claimsman _____

(Answers on page 167.)

Lesson 20

ROOT: CLUD, CLUS, CLAUS, CLOSE
MEANING: shut, close

Example
include
occlusor
exclude
inclusive
conclusive

Meaning
to take in
an organ which closes
to shut out
containing almost everything
final, shutting door to additional information

Test Yourself

Define the following words.

1. seclude _____
2. occlude _____
3. conclude _____
4. preclude _____
5. recluse _____
6. exclusive _____
7. clause _____

(Answers on page 167.)

Lesson 21

ROOT: COGN
MEANING: know

Example
cognizant
prognosticator
cognoscente
cognition

Meaning
knowing, aware
one who can predict
one having special knowledge
the act of knowing

Test Yourself

Define the following words.

1. cognize _____

2. prognosticate _____

Recognizing Words

Select the word that is *closest* in meaning to the key word.

3. recognize   a. state over   b. ignore
                   c. know again   d. unable
4. incognito   a. well-known   b. viewed
                   c. perceive   d. disguised
5. cognitive   a. electrical   b. knowing
                   c. feeling   d. stating
6. diagnose   a. will   b. classify
                   c. fail   d. preliminary

(Answers on page 167.)

Lesson 22

ROOT: CORP
MEANING: body

Example — **Meaning**
corpse — a dead body
corporate — combined into one body
corporealist — one interested only in material things
corps — an organization
corpus — entire body, complete collection

Test Yourself

Define the following words.

1. corporeal   _____
2. incorporate   _____
3. corporation   _____
4. corpulent   _____
5. corpuscle   _____
6. corporator   _____

(Answers on page 167.)

Lesson 23

ROOT: COURT
MEANING: pertaining to the court (sovereign's residence)

Example	Meaning
court	a meeting place, king's assembly
courtesy	excellent manners
court martial	trial of military law
discourteously	rudely
courtliness	elegant behavior at king's court

Test Yourself

Define the following words.

1. courtly _____
2. discourtesy _____
3. courtesan _____
4. courtship _____
5. courtyard _____

(Answers on page 167.)

Lesson 24

ROOT: CREAT
MEANING: create

Example
create
recreation
procreate
creant
uncreative

Meaning
bring into existence
act of refreshing, enjoyment
to give birth to
creating
unimaginative

Test Yourself

Define the following words.

1. creative _____
2. procreative _____
3. creation _____
4. recreate _____
5. miscreant _____
6. creativity _____
7. creature _____
8. creator _____

(Answers on page 168.)

Lesson 25

ROOT: CRED
MEANING: believe, trust

Example
credo
discredit
credulity
credit

Meaning
a belief
destroy reputation
willingness to believe too readily
trustworthiness

Test Yourself
Define the following words.

1. credence _____
2. creditable _____
3. credential _____
4. credit agency _____
5. discreditable _____

Recognizing Words
In the following examples, select the word that is *closest* in meaning to the key word.

6. creditor
   a. ower
   b. sealant
   c. trust
   d. lender
7. incredible
   a. believable
   b. stunning
   c. implausible
   d. faultless
8. credulous
   a. disappointing
   b. effortless
   c. trusting
   d. unassuming
9. accredit
   a. approve
   b. check
   c. finance
   d. war
10. creed
    a. renegade
    b. fulfillment
    c. startle
    d. belief

(Answers on page 168.)

Lesson 26

ROOT: CYCL, CYCLO
MEANING: circle, circular, wheel, ring

Example
cycle
cyclopedic
encyclical

cyclone

Meaning
a round of years
to be like an encyclopedia
letter addressed to all individuals in a group often from the pope to bishops
atmospheric disturbance with circular winds

Test Yourself

Define the following words.

1. cyclic _____
2. cyclometer _____
3. encyclopedia _____
4. cyclist _____
5. cyclostome _____
6. cyclops _____
7. bicycle _____
8. unicycle _____
9. cycloid _____
10. cyclorama _____

(Answers on page 168.)

Lesson 27

ROOT: DENT, DONT
MEANING: tooth

Example
dental
dentist
dentigerous
denticate
dentilated

Meaning
relating to teeth
one who cares for teeth
having teeth
to chew
toothed

Test Yourself

Define the following words.

1. dentin _____
2. orthodontist _____
3. dentoid _____
4. denture _____
5. dentition _____
6. dentiform _____
7. periodontist _____

(Answers on page 168.)

Lesson 28

ROOT: DICT
MEANING: state, say, declare, speak

Example
dictate
dictionary
predicate
ditto

Meaning
command
reference book containing words
to affirm
the same again

Test Yourself
Define the following words.

1. malediction   _____
2. dictator   _____
3. indict   _____
4. indicator   _____
5. dicker   _____

Recognizing Words

Select the word that is *closest* in meaning to the key word.

6. contradict   a. talk to   b. will
                  c. alter   d. speak against
7. indicate   a. accuse   b. point out
                 c. falter   d. triumph
8. prediction   a. anger   b. contrition
                   c. prophecy   d. harassment
9. edict   a. correction   b. disclaimer
             c. decree   d. fault
10. dictum   a. pronouncement   b. energy
               c. alarm   d. vote

(Answers on page 169.)

Lesson 29

ROOT: DORM
MEANING: sleep

Example
dormitory
dormient
dormeuse

Meaning
building for living or sleeping
sleeping
woman's cap

Test Yourself

Define the following words.

1. dormer _____
2. dormant _____
3. dormancy _____
4. dormitive _____
5. dorm _____

(Answers on page 169.)

Lesson 30

ROOT: DROME, DROMOS
MEANING: run

Example | **Meaning**
dromos | a race track in ancient Greece
dromond | fast sailing vessel from middle ages
hippodromist | circus rider
syndrome | a group of symptoms

Test Yourself

Define the following words.

1. dromedary _____
2. androme _____
3. hippodrome _____
4. motordrome _____
5. prodrome _____
6. dromometer _____
7. dromograph _____

(Answers on page 169.)

Lesson 31

ROOT: DUC, DUCE, DUCT
MEANING: lead

Example
educate
induce
aqueduct

misconduct
reduce

Meaning
to teach, lead away from ignorance
to lead into
a structure for carrying flowing water
bad behavior
to lead to a lower position

Recognizing Words

Match the words with their correct definitions.

1. abduct
2. deduce
3. duce
4. viaduct
5. produce
6. conduct
7. seduce
8. traduce
9. reduction
10. inductile

a. leader
b. unyielding, not easily lead
c. bring forth
d. lowering
e. take away by force
f. to lead
g. slander
h. to determine the course of
i. lead astray
j. bridge

(Answers on page 169.)

Lesson 32

ROOT: ENDO
MEANING: within

Example
endocrine
endogeny
endotoxin
endoparasite

endogamy

Meaning
any internal secretion
growth from within
toxin of internal origin
parasite living within the internal organs of its host
marriage within a specific tribe or group

Test Yourself

Define the following words.

1. endogastric
2. endosteal
3. endoscope
4. endomorph
5. endosperm
6. endophyte
7. endocardial
8. endocarp

(Answers on page 169.)

Lesson 33

ROOT: FAC, FACT
MEANING: make

Example
fact
malefactor
factotum
factory

Meaning
a deed
criminal
versatile person
place where things are made

Test Yourself
Define the following words.

1. faculty _____
2. satisfaction _____
3. factor _____
4. facile _____
5. facility _____

Recognizing Words

In the following examples, select the word that is *closest* in meaning to the key word.

6. faction
   a. center   b. group
   c. around   d. alone
7. factive
   a. pleasant   b. annoying
   c. causing   d. false
8. facsimile
   a. determination b. copy
   c. awareness   d. union
9. putrefaction
   a. rotting   b. age
   c. weirdness   d. content
10. dissatisfaction
   a. discontent   b. fault
   c. knowledge   d. heaviness

(*Answers on page 169.*)

Lesson 34

ROOT: FEDER, FID, FIDE
MEANING: trust, have faith

Example
infidelity
confide
federal
fiducial

Meaning
without faith
to have trust in someone
an alliance, united
based on having trust

Test Yourself

Define the following words.

1. federation
2. infidel
3. perfidious
4. confederate
5. bonafide
6. confidence
7. affidavit
8. fiduciary
9. affiance
10. confederacy

(Answers on page 170.)

Lesson 35

ROOT: FECT, FIC
MEANING: make, do

Example
affect
magnificent
deficiency
disinfect
confection

Meaning
make an impression upon
made grandly or attractively
something lacking
make free from germs
a sweet; act of making sweets

Test Yourself

Define the following words.

1. beneficiary _____
2. proficient _____
3. personification _____
4. defective _____
5. affectation _____
6. versification _____
7. sufficient _____
8. identification _____
9. effect _____
10. perfect _____

(Answers on page 170.)

Lesson 36

ROOT: FER
MEANING: bear, carry, bring, yield

Example   **Meaning**
fertile   bearing fruit
transfer   bring from place to place
defer   to yield, put off
offer   to present, bring forth
odiferous   having a smell

Test Yourself

Match the appropriate words in each column.

1. confer
2. differ
3. infer
4. proffer
5. refer
6. suffer
7. conifer
8. afferent

a. to conclude by reason
b. to bear pain
c. bestow upon
d. cone bearing
e. unlike, bear apart
f. bearing inward
g. bring attention to
h. to offer

(Answers on page 170.)

Lesson 37

ROOT: FIL
MEANING: thread

Example
filament
filium
filamentous
file

Meaning
a threadlike wire
a thread
full of thread
to arrange in order

Test Yourself

Define the following words.

1. filigree
2. filature
3. filiform
4. filar
5. filaria
6. profile

(Answers on page 170.)

Lesson 38

ROOT: **FIN**
MEANING: end

Example
final
definitive
financial
finis

Meaning
relating to the end
conclusive
relating to money
the end or conclusion

Test Yourself

Define the following words.

1. finale _____
2. fine _____
3. finial _____
4. finite _____
5. infinite _____
6. define _____
7. fin de siècle _____
8. finalist _____

(Answers on page 170.)

Lesson 39

ROOT: **FIX**
MEANING: fix (A multi-purpose root, with multiple meanings.)

Different Meanings of Fix
fix   make stable
fix   repair
fix   attract the eye
fix   narcotic injection
fix   establish

Test Yourself
Define the following words.

1. fixer　_____
2. affix　_____
3. transfix　_____
4. fixative　_____
5. fixation　_____
6. fix　_____
7. fixed　_____
8. fixture　_____

(Answers on page 171.)

Lesson 40

ROOT: FLECT, FLEX
MEANING: bend

Example | Meaning
flex — to bend
reflect — bend back a light, to think about
flexible — able to bend

Test Yourself

Define the following words.

1. genuflect _____
2. flexor _____
3. flexile _____
4. flexography _____

Recognizing Words

Match the appropriate word with its correct definition.

5. deflect
6. inflection
7. reflective
8. reflector
9. flexuous
10. flexed

a. rise and fall of voice
b. bent at the knee
c. bend away
d. having many bends or curves
e. a device that bends back light
f. having the ability to reflect

(Answers on page 171.)

Lesson 41

ROOT: FLU, FLUC, FLUV, FLUX
MEANING: flowing

Example **Meaning**
fluid   a flowing liquid
flux   continuous change

Test Yourself
Define the following words.

1. influx   _____
2. fluent   _____
3. superfluous   _____
4. confluence   _____
5. effluvium   _____

Recognizing Words

For the following words, select the word that is closest in meaning to the original word.

6. flume
   a. white hot   b. passage for water
   c. airborne   d. birdlike
7. fluctuate
   a. end   b. solder
   c. ebb and flow in waves   d. harden
8. fluviose
   a. verbose   b. freely flowing
   c. fat   d. weighty
9. affluent
   a. prosperous   b. unhappy
   c. thrilled   d. tired
10. flue
    a. passageway b. illness
    c. aloft   d. untried

(Answers on page 171.)

Lesson 42

ROOT: FUM
MEANING: smoke

Example | **Meaning**
fume (n) | smoke, state of anger, odor
fume (v) | to express anger; to give off fumes
fumigate | to apply fumes (to destroy vermin)

Test Yourself

Define the following words.

1. fumigant _____
2. fumarole _____
3. fumatorium _____
4. fumy _____
5. fumigator _____

Recognizing Words

Match the definitions in the right column with the words in the left column.

6. fumigation
7. defume
8. fumacious
9. perfume
10. fumaduct

a. liking fumes or smoke
b. unsmoke, removal of fumes or smoke
c. the act of applying or making smoke
d. chimney, opening for smoke
e. pleasant odor

(Answers on page 171.)

Lesson 43

ROOT: GEN
MEANING: beget, bear, kind, race

Example
gene

engender
genesis

Meaning
substance that transmits hereditary characteristics
to beget, bring into being
the beginning of something

Test Yourself
Define the following words.

1. gentility _____
2. gentle _____
3. gentry _____
4. genus _____
5. genial _____

Recognizing Words
Match the definitions in the right column with the words in the left column.

6. generate
7. genetic
8. congenital
9. congener
10. eugenics

a. relating to the origin, development or cause of something
b. dating from birth, inborn, with one at birth
c. science dealing with improvement of hereditary characteristics
d. to bring into existence
e. one related to another

(Answers on page 171.)

Lesson 44

ROOT: GERM
MEANING: vital part, bud

Example
germ
germicide
germinate

Meaning
seed, main living substance
substance that kills life
to sprout, grow

Test Yourself

Define the following words.

1. germination   _____
2. germ proof   _____
3. germinable   _____
4. germy   _____
5. germane   _____

Recognizing Words

Match the definitions in the right column with the words in the left column.

6. germule
7. germfree
8. germless
9. germiparity
10. germinal

a. small germ
b. reproduction of germs
c. free of microorganisms
d. relating to germs
e. free of germs of life

(Answers on page 172.)

Lesson 45

ROOT: GEST, GER
MEANING: bear, carry

Example | Meaning
ingest — carry into
gestate — to carry or bear during pregnancy
gesture — the use of motions as a form of expression
belligerent — waging war

Test Yourself

Define the following words.

1. gesticulate _____
2. gesticular _____
3. congest _____
4. gestant _____
5. gestic _____

Recognizing Words

Match the definitions in the right column with the words in the left column.

6. congestive
7. gestation
8. digest
9. gestative
10. suggestion

a. make food absorbable in the body
b. causing overcrowding
c. having to do with gestation
d. process by which one thought carries over to another
e. period of pregnancy (carrying)

(Answers on page 172.)

Lesson 46

ROOT: GNOSI
MEANING: know

Example
agnostic

diagnosis

incognito

Meaning
one who says that knowledge of the existence of God is unknowable

the art or act of knowing (particularly diseases)

unknown

Test Yourself
Define the following words.

1. cognosce _____
2. ignorant _____
3. prognosis _____
4. cognizance _____
5. recognize _____

Recognizing Words
Match the definitions in the right hand column with the words in the left column.

6. prognostic
7. ignoramus
8. agnosy
9. diagnostician
10. cognizable

a. a person who finds knowledge about something
b. state of not knowing
c. a person who lacks knowledge
d. foretelling
e. has the ability to be known

(Answers on page 172.)

Lesson 47

ROOT: GRAD, GRED, GRESS
MEANING: step, degree, walk

Example
digress
egress
gradual

Meaning
step aside, leave the subject
exit
make headway by means of small steps

Test Yourself

Define the following words.

1. progress _____
2. graduate _____
3. transgress _____
4. aggression _____
5. retrograde _____

Recognizing Words

Match the definitions in the right column with the words in the left column.

6. regression
7. degrade
8. degree
9. ingredient
10. congress

a. substance needed to follow steps of a recipe
b. the act of going back
c. a step in advancement
d. to put a step lower
e. a walking together, gathering

(Answers on page 172.)

Lesson 48

ROOT: GRAPH, GRAM
MEANING: write

Example	**Meaning**
calligraphy	writing that is elegant
homograph	two words with the same spelling, but different meanings
telegram	a communication by telegraph machine

Test Yourself

Define the following words.

1. lithography _____
2. mimeograph _____
3. orthography _____
4. phonograph _____
5. geography _____

Recognizing Words

Match the definitions in the right column with the words in the left column.

6. graphomania
7. holograph
8. graphic
9. telegraph
10. monograph

a. a mania for writing
b. being written
c. electrical transmission of letters
d. an article written on a single subject
e. something written solely by the signer

(Answers on page 172.)

Lesson 49

ROOT: GRAT
MEANING: thankful, pleasing, giving pleasure

Example
ingrate
congratulate
gratulatory

Meaning
one who is ungrateful
rejoice together with
possessing quality of pleasing

Test Yourself

Define the following words.

1. gratuity   _____
2. ingratitude   _____
3. gratify   _____
4. grateful   _____
5. gratitude   _____

Recognizing Words

Match the definitions in the right column with the words in the left column.

6. gratuitant
7. congratulation
8. gratuitous
9. ingratiate
10. ungrateful

a. not thankful for favors
b. something not called for
c. gain favor by effort
d. act of congratulating
e. one receiving favor or pleasure

(Answers on page 173.)

Lesson 50

ROOT: GRAV
MEANING: weighty, heavy

Example | **Meaning**
aggravate | to make heavier, increase
grave | weighty
gravely | heavily

Test Yourself
Define the following words.

1. gravitate _____
2. gravity _____
3. gravimetry _____
4. gravitative _____
5. graviton _____

Recognizing Words

Match the definitions in the right column with the words in the left column.

6. gravimeter
7. gravimetric
8. gravific
9. gravitational
10. gravid

a. relating to measurement by weight
b. instrument used to measure specific gravity
c. having to do with the tendency of objects to fall to earth
d. weight producing
e. pregnant

(Answers on page 173.)

Lesson 51

ROOT: GREG
MEANING: crowd, mob, flock, herd, group

Example
congregate
aggregation
gregarian

Meaning
to flock together
a grouping
member of the group or herd

Test Yourself

Define the following words.

1. gregarious   _____
2. aggregate   _____
3. egregious   _____
4. segregate   _____
5. congregative   _____

Recognizing Words

Match the definitions in the right column with the words in the left column.

6. aggregative
7. antisegregationist
8. congregation
9. aggregable
10. congregational

a. a group acting as one mind
b. tendency to form into a group
c. having to do with a crowd or flock
d. one against segregation
e. able to be a group

(Answers on page 173.)

Lesson 52

ROOT: HAB, HABIT
MEANING: live, have

Example　**Meaning**
habitat　natural living area of plant or animal
inhabit　to incorporate an area of one's living space
habit　manner of behavior

Test Yourself

Define the following words.

1. habitation _____
2. habituate   _____
3. habitant   _____
4. cohabit   _____
5. habitual   _____

Recognizing Words

Match the definitions in the right column with the words in the left column.

6. habiliments
7. habilitate
8. rehabilitate
9. habitual
10. inhabitant

a. to make ready for life again
b. furnishings of life
c. having to do with habit or custom
d. to dress, to furnish
e. one living in a certain area

(Answers on page 173.)

Lesson 53

ROOT: HELI, HELIO
MEANING: sun

Example
heliotherapy
helical
helium

Meaning
using the sun to cure an ailment
spiral, winding circles
a light, nonflammable gas

Test Yourself

Define the following words.

1. heliograph _____
2. heliogram _____
3. heliocentric _____
4. heliophyte _____
5. helioscope _____

Recognizing Words

Match the definitions in the right column with the words in the left column.

6. heliotrope
7. heliophobic
8. heliosis
9. heliochromy
10. heliogy

a. the study of the sun
b. color photography
c. sunburn or sunstroke
d. fear of the sun
e. a plant which turns toward the sun

(Answers on page 173.)

Lesson 54

ROOT: HEMA, HEMO
MEANING: blood

Example | **Meaning**
hematology | branch of biology that deals with the blood
hemoid | like blood
hemophilia | bleeding which cannot be controlled

Test Yourself

Define the following words.

1. hemal _____
2. hemostat _____
3. hemotose _____
4. hemocyte _____
5. hemoglobin _____

Recognizing Words

Match the definitions in the right column with the words in the left column.

6. hemogastric
7. hemorrhage
8. hemodialysis
9. hemodynamic
10. hematic

a. relating to blood circulation
b. containing blood
c. intense bleeding
d. having to do with bleeding into the stomach
e. purification of blood by dialysis

(Answers on page 174.)

Lesson 55

ROOT: HYDR, HYDRA, HYDRO
MEANING: water

Example **Meaning**
hydrostat   instrument used to regulate the flow of water
dehydrate   to remove water

Test Yourself
Define the following words.

1. hydrophobia   _____
2. hydroplane   _____
3. hydropropulsion _____
4. hydroscope   _____
5. anhydrous   _____

Recognizing Words

Match the definitions in the right column with the words in the left column.

6. hydrate   a. a plant so named because it needs enormous amounts of water
7. hydrangea   b. water plus one other element
8. hydrophone   c. use of water to treat an ailment
9. hydrotherapy d. an instrument used for listening to water in pipes
10. hydrosphere e. water vapor as it surrounds the earth

(Answers on page 174.)

Lesson 56

ROOT: HYPNO, HYPN
MEANING: sleep

Example
hypnotic
hypnophobia

Meaning
soporific, causing to sleep
fear of sleep

Test Yourself
Define the following words.

1. hypnophobic _____
2. hypnotism _____
3. hypnoid _____
4. hypnotizable _____
5. hypnoidal _____

Recognizing Words
Match the definitions in the right column with the words in the left column.

6. hypnoanalysis
7. hypnosis
8. hypnotist
9. hypnagogic
10. hypnogenesis

a. one who practices hypnosis
b. a state of sleep-like behavior brought on by suggestion
c. induction of hypnotic state of being
d. relating to drowsiness
e. treatment of mental disease by hypnosis

(Answers on page 174.)

Lesson 57

ROOT: INTELLECT, INTELLIG
MEANING: ability to think or know

Example
intelligent
intellect
intellectual

Meaning
having the ability to think and know
the power of knowing or thinking
relating to the use of the intellect

Test Yourself
Define the following words.

1. intelligible _____
2. intelligence _____
3. unintelligent _____
4. intelligentsia _____
5. intellectualist _____

Recognizing Words
Match the definitions in the right column with the words in the left column.

6. intelligently
7. intellectualize
8. unintelligible
9. intelligibility
10. intelligencer

a. not to be known or understood
b. spy, secret agent
c. in an intelligent way
d. the quality of being intelligible
e. to organize into a knowledgeable order

(Answers on page 174.)

Lesson 58

ROOT: JAC, JECT
MEANING: lie, throw

Example
conjecture
interjection

ejection

Meaning
to surmise, formulate an opinion
a word thrown between other words (literally)
a throwing out

Test Yourself
Define the following words.

1. eject
2. inject
3. conject
4. projection
5. reject

Recognizing Words
Match the definitions in the right column with the words in the left column.

6. dejected
7. dejection
8. introjection
9. objection

10. ejaculate

a. state of being cast down
b. refusal to accept
c. to throw out
d. the idea of throwing oneself into a cause
e. cast down

(Answers on page 174.)

Lesson 59

ROOT: JOIN, JUNC, JUG
MEANING: join

Example
conjoin
adjunctive
subjunctive

Meaning
bring together, unite
likely to cause a joining
of, relating to

Test Yourself

Define the following words.

1. adjoining _____
2. junctive _____
3. enjoin _____
4. disjoin _____
5. conjuncture _____

Recognizing Words

Match the definitions in the right column with the words in the left column.

6. conjunction
7. conjoiner
8. conjugal
9. conjunctiva
10. junction

a. part of speech which joins words and/or phrases
b. related to the married state
c. someone who or something that joins things
d. a place of joining or coming together
e. mucus membrane lining inner-eye surface

(Answers on page 175.)

Lesson 60

ROOT: JUD, JUDI, JUDIC
MEANING: judge

Example	**Meaning**
prejudice	discrimination, bias
judicious	showing sound judgment
adjudicate	to resolve by decree from judge

Test Yourself

Define the following words.

1. judicial _____
2. judge _____
3. judgment _____
4. prejudicial _____
5. judicable _____

Recognizing Words

Match the definitions in the right column with the words in the left column.

6. judiciary
7. judicator
8. abjudicate
9. injudicious
10. unprejudicial

a. system of courts of law
b. not having sound judgment
c. without being prejudiced or biased
d. to refuse to judge a case
e. a judge

(Answers on page 175.)

Lesson 61

ROOT: JUR
MEANING: swear

Example **Meaning**
jury   a body of persons sworn to inquire and deliberate according to an accepted body of law
juror   member of a jury

Test Yourself
Define the following words.

1. jurisprudence _____
2. perjury _____
3. jurisdiction _____
4. abjure _____
5. conjure _____

Recognizing Words

Match the definitions in the right column with the words in the left column.

6. injury   a. one having a complete knowledge of law
7. jurist   b. false swearing
8. juridical   c. of or relating to the administration of law
9. perjure   d. a member of a jury
10. jural   e. a wrong

(Answers on page 175.)

Lesson 62

ROOT: LABOR
MEANING: to work

Example
labor (n)

laboratory

belabor

Meaning
work done for profit, especially work requiring difficult effort

a place where scientific experiments are performed

to work on to absurd lengths

Test Yourself

Define the following words.

1. labor (v) _____
2. belabored _____
3. laborsaving _____
4. laborer _____
5. laborite _____
6. labored _____
7. laborious _____

(Answers on page 175.)

Lesson 63

ROOT: LAV, LU,
MEANING: wash, clean with water

Example **Meaning**
launder to wash
lava natural abrasive igneous rock often used as cleaning powder
lavatory a place designed as a washing area

Test Yourself

Define the following words.

1. lavabo   _____
2. deluge   _____
3. dilute   _____
4. dilution _____
5. lave   _____

Recognizing Words

Match the definitions in the right column with the words in the left column.

6. diluval
7. alluvium
8. ablution
9. lavish
10. lavation

a. flowing like water, luxurious
b. relating to a flood
c. a cleansing
d. an act of washing
e. something deposited by water

(Answers on page 175.)

Lesson 64

ROOT: LEG
MEANING: law

Example
legist
illegal
legacy

Meaning
ambassador
against the law
a gift left to be bestowed under administrators of the law

Test Yourself

Define the following words.

1. legitimate
2. legislator
3. legator
4. legate (v)
5. legislate

Recognizing Words

Match the definitions in the right column with the words in the left column.

6. legalistic
7. legislation
8. legalize
9. illegality
10. legatee

a. enactment of the law by legislator
b. one receiving a gift of legacy
c. make law
d. according to the letter of the law
e. a state of being unlawful

(Answers on page 176.)

Lesson 65

ROOT: LITER
MEANING: letters

Example
literacy
literary
literature

Meaning
the condition of being educated
having to do with books and writing
books, writing

Test Yourself
Define the following words.

1. literalism _____
2. illiterate _____
3. literal _____
4. alliteration _____
5. transliterate _____

Recognizing Words

Match the definitions in the right column with the words in the left column.

6. alliterator
7. literatus
8. literatim
9. litterateur
10. obliterate

a. letter for letter
b. a professional writer
c. well-educated person
d. to make letters obscure
e. one using alliteration

(Answers on page 176.)

Lesson 66

ROOT: LIBER, LIVER
MEANING: free

Example   **Meaning**
liberty   freedom
liberate   to free or make free
liberal   having to do with freedom

Test Yourself

Define the following words.

1. liberalism   _____
2. liberticide   _____
3. deliver   _____
4. liberalize   _____
5. illiberal   _____

Recognizing Words

Match the definitions in the right column with the words in the left column.

6. liberality
7. deliverance
8. liberator
9. libertine
10. delivery

a. one who is without morals
b. broad-mindedness
c. freedom
d. condition of being freed
e. one who makes freedom possible

(Answers on page 176.)

Lesson 67

ROOT: LIC
MEANING: permit

Example
license
licit
illicit

Meaning
a permit, freedom to act
permitted, lawful
illegal

Test Yourself

Define the following words.

1. licentiation _____
2. licensed _____
3. licensure _____
4. illicitness _____
5. licentious _____

Recognizing Words

Match the definitions in the right column with the words in the left column.

6. unlicensed
7. illicitly
8. licentiously
9. licensor
10. licensee

a. person authorized to distribute licenses
b. unlawfully
c. not permitted
d. person granted the permit or license
e. immorally

(Answers on page 176.)

Lesson 68

ROOT: LOC
MEANING: place

Example
local
locate
locality

Meaning
relating to a particular place
to find where an object or person is
a particular place

Test Yourself

Define the following words.

1. locale
2. dislocate
3. locomotive
4. locus
5. locomotivity

Recognizing Words

Match the definitions in the right column with the words in the left column.

6. dislocator
7. relocate
8. allocate
9. relocation
10. dislocatory

a. one who causes an object to be removed from place
b. causing something to be removed from place
c. the action of putting something back into place
d. to put back into place
e. to assign

(Answers on page 176.)

Lesson 69

ROOT: LOG, LOGO
MEANING: word

Example
logic
logical
logographer

Meaning
science of speech and reasoning
having to do with logic
speech writer

Test Yourself

Define the following words.

1. travelogue _____
2. logician _____
3. monologue _____
4. logistics _____
5. logolatry _____

Recognizing Words

Match the definitions in the right column with the words in the left column.

6. logomania
7. eulogy
8. logorrhea
9. logomachy
10. logogram

a. excessive wordiness
b. possessing a mania for talking
c. praise
d. a letter representing an entire word
e. a dispute over words

(Answers on page 177.)

Lesson 70

ROOT: LOQUI, LOQU
MEANING: speak

Example
loquacious
obloquy
colloquial

Meaning
excessively talkative
speaking condemnatory messages
informal speaking, using local slang vocabulary

Test Yourself

Define the following words.

1. soliloquy
2. ventriloquist
3. eloquence
4. loquacity
5. loquent

Recognizing Words

Match the definitions in the right column with the words in the left column

6. soliloquize
7. obliquious
8. interlocution
9. interloctor
10. eloquent

a. conversation
b. characterized by obloquy
c. conversationalist
d. communicating with ease and skill
e. to talk to oneself

(Answers on page 177.)

Lesson 71

ROOT: LUC, LUM, LUN, LUS, LUX
MEANING: light

Example / Meaning

pellucid — easily "brought to light" or understood

lucidity — the capability of appearing "full of light" or bright

translucent — partially admitting light

Test Yourself

Define the following words.

1. elucidate _____
2. illusion _____
3. lucid _____
4. lucubrator _____
5. lumen _____

Recognizing Words

Match the definitions in the right column with the words in the left column.

6. illusory
7. luculent
8. lucubrate
9. luminescence
10. luminiferous

a. the act of "bringing things into the light" or studying to acquire knowledge
b. brightness
c. giving light, producing light
d. based on illusion
e. laborious study

(Answers on page 177.)

Lesson 72

ROOT: MAGN
MEANING: great

Example
magnitude
magnate

magnanimous

Meaning
greatness of size or number
a person of greatness or influence
showing greatness of heart or spirit

Test Yourself
Define the following words.

1. magnificent _____
2. magnolia _____
3. magnificence _____
4. magnify _____
5. magna charta _____

Recognizing Words
Match the definitions in the right column with the words in the left column.

6. magnifico
7. magna cum laude
8. magnum opus
9. magnum
10. magnificat

a. a person of great or high rank
b. a song proclaiming greatness
c. large wine bottle
d. with great distinction
e. a great work

(Answers on page 177.)

Lesson 73

ROOT: MAN, MANU
MEANING: by hand

Example
manuscript (n)
manufacture

manacle

Meaning
a written composition
the act of making products by hand
handcuff

Test Yourself
Define the following words.

1. manifest   _____
2. manipulate _____
3. maneuver   _____
4. manual   _____
5. manufactory _____

Recognizing Words

Match the definitions in the right column with the words in the left column.

6. manicure
7. manumit
8. manipulation
9. legerdemain
10. manuduction

a. the manual operation of something
b. to care for the hand
c. light-handed magic tricks
d. free from slavery
e. a leading by the hand

(*Answers on page 177.*)

Lesson 74

ROOT: MAR, MARI, MER
MEANING: sea, pool

Example
marine (adj.)
maritime

submarine

Meaning
having to do with the sea
having to do with sea trade and navigation
a boat capable of operating on or below the seas

Test Yourself

Define the following words.

1. marine (n.) _____
2. marinorama _____
3. mermaid _____
4. mere _____
5. marsh _____

Recognizing Words

Match the definitions in the right column with the words in the left column.

6. mariner
7. marina
8. aquamarine
9. marsh
10. marine biologist

a. a place that offers boats protection from the open sea
b. a blue or blue-green beryl
c. an area of soft, wet land
d. a navigator of a ship
e. a student of sea life

(Answers on page 178.)

Lesson 75

ROOT: MATER, MATR
MEANING: mother

Example
maternal
matron
matricide

Meaning
derived or inherited from a mother
a dignified married woman
the killing of a mother by her child

Test Yourself
Define the following words.

1. matrix _____
2. alma mater _____
3. matrilineal _____
4. matrimony _____
5. maternity _____

Recognizing Words

Match the definitions in the right column with the words in the left column.

6. matriarch
7. mater
8. matripotestal
9. matronymic
10. matriculate

a. having to do with powers exercised by a mother
b. Latin word for mother
c. a name derived from the mother's name
d. a woman who rules a group, family, or tribe
e. to enroll as a member of a school

(Answers on page 178.)

Lesson 76

ROOT: MED
MEANING: half, between, middle

Example
mediate
median

Meaning
to act as a middle man
a middle place or value

Test Yourself

Define the following words.

1. mediocre _____
2. immediate _____
3. medial   _____
4. medieval _____

Recognizing Words

Read the following paragraph and fill in each blank with the correct answer choice. Definitions are in parentheses.

a. mediglacial (positioned between two glaciers)
b. intermeddle (a go-between)
c. intermediary (being in the middle)
d. Mediterranean (literally between the lands; i.e., the sea between the lands)
e. mediate (reconcile)

I once knew a businessman who was hired to travel to an Italian coastal city. He enjoyed his stay on the shores of the ____5____. His job was to ____6____ between two powerful, but bickering parties interested in exchanging money for fossils found in a ____7____ area in the very cold section of northern Russia. His job as ____8____ allowed him to ____9____ two very powerful businessmen. His trip proved to be relaxing, yet interesting.

(Answers on page 178.)

Lesson 77

ROOT: MEGA, MEGAL
MEANING: large, great, million

Example
magaphone

megalomania

Meaning
an instrument for making sound greater
a mind disorder characterized by delusions of grandeur

Test Yourself

Define the following words.

1. megacycle _____
2. megaton _____
3. megalopolis _____
4. megapod _____
5. megalith _____

Recognizing Words

Match the definitions in the right column with the words in the left column.

6. megalosaurus   a. a large meat-eating dinosaur
7. megohm   b. enlarged; easily visible to the naked eye
8. acromegaly   c. having large teeth
9. megadont   d. disease which causes enlargement of the face, hands and feet
10. megascopic   e. 1,000,000 ohms

(Answers on page 178.)

Lesson 78

ROOT: MEMOR
MEANING: remember

Example
memorize
memory
memorable

Meaning
to learn by heart
the power or ability to remember
worthy of remembering

Test Yourself
Define the following words.

1. commemorate _____
2. memorabilia _____
3. memoir _____
4. memorandum _____
5. memo _____

Recognizing Words
Match the definitions in the right column with the words in the left column.

6. memoirist
7. memento
8. memorial
9. commemoration
10. memorandize

a. a ceremony serving as a memorial
b. writer of memoirs
c. souvenir
d. the act of writing a memorandum
e. something that serves to cause people to remember a person or an event

(Answers on page 178.)

Lesson 79

ROOT: METER, METR
MEANING: measure

Example
meter

metric

Meaning
basic metric unit of length measurement

of or relating to the meter, decimal system weights, and measure

Test Yourself

Define the following words.

1. barometer _____
2. symmetry _____
3. geometry _____
4. altimeter _____

Recognizing Words

Match the definitions in the right column with the words in the left column.

5. trigonometry

6. diameter

7. pedometer

8. parameter

a. device used to measure walking distance

b. a straight line that divides a circle into two equal halves

c. a given; a characteristic factor

d. a branch of mathematics dealing with properties of triangles, and their applications

(Answers on page 179.)

Lesson 80

ROOT: MICRO
MEANING: very small

Example
microscope

microbe

Meaning
a device used to allow observance of very small objects

a very small living organism

Test Yourself
Define the following words.

1. micron _____
2. microcosm _____
3. microfilm _____
4. microbial _____
5. microcopy _____

Recognizing Words
Match the definitions in the right column with the words in the left column.

6. micrometer
7. microcyte
8. micromania
9. microbicide

10. microlith

a. a small stone tool
b. something which destroys microbes
c. a small red blood cell
d. mind disorder which results in the illusion that one's body has become very small
e. device used to measure very small distances

(Answers on page 179.)

Lesson 81

ROOT: MIGRA
MEANING: wander

Example
migrate
immigrate

Meaning
to move from one place to another
to come into a foreign country

Test Yourself
Define the following words.
1. transmigration _____
2. immigratory _____
3. emigrative _____

Recognizing Words

Read the following paragraph and fill in each blank with the correct answer choice. Definitions are in parentheses.

a. migratorial (having to do with wandering)
b. immigration (the act of immigrating)
c. migratory (wandering)
d. emigration (the act of emigrating)
e. emigrees (person forced to emigrate)

I'm not too sure about existing ____4____ laws, but they must be reviewed. American servicemen left thousands of offspring in southeast Asia, and, due to living conditions prevalent in that area, many of these older children consider ____5____. They would love to grow up in America. In Vietnam, for example, the existing government virtually ignores them, and would gladly force them to be ____6____. Their existence in Southeast Asia is constantly ____7____ because, according to the laws of those countries, they are not permitted to live in permanent homes. They exist clinging to hopes that America will put an end to their ____8____ lifestyles.

(Answers on page 179.)

Lesson 82

ROOT: MISS, MIT
MEANING: send, convey

Example
mission

missive
admit

Meaning
a task which a person or a group is sent to complete
a note or letter
to allow to enter

Test Yourself

Define the following words.

1. commission _____
2. dismiss _____
3. remit _____
4. permit _____
5. transmit _____

Recognizing Words

Match the definitions in the right column with the words in the left column.

6. emit
7. missionary
8. dismissal
9. admission
10. remission

a. a person sent by a church to propagate its faith
b. the granting of an argument
c. to send off or out
d. the act of sending away
e. postponement

(Answers on page 179.)

Lesson 83

ROOT: MOB, MOT, MOV
MEANING: move

Example
mobile
moveable
motion

Meaning
able to move or be moved
able to move
instance of moving

Test Yourself
Define the following words.

1. motor   _____
2. motive _____
3. promote _____
4. demote _____
5. locomotion _____

Recognizing Words

Match the definitions in the right column with the words in the left column.

6. removable
7. immovable
8. automobile
9. mobilize
10. mobility

a. to move or make able to move
b. able to be moved away
c. inability to be moved
d. the ability to move
e. a self-propelled vehicle

(Answers on page 180.)

Lesson 84

ROOT: MONSTR, MONSTRI, MUST
MEANING: show

Example
monster
demonstrate
muster

Meaning
freak; malformed being
to show
to gather together; collect

Test Yourself
Define the following words.

1. demonstration _____
2. remonstrative _____
3. demonstrational _____
4. remonstration _____
5. monstrosity _____

Recognizing Words
Match the definitions in the right column with the words in the left column.

6. monstrance
7. monstrous
8. monstriferous
9. monstrification
10. musterer

a. monster-like, abnormal
b. producing monsters
c. process of developing into a monster
d. vessel for holding the Host in Catholic ritual
e. collector, gatherer

(Answers on page 180.)

Lesson 85

ROOT: MORI, MORS, MORT
MEANING: death

Example | **Meaning**
mortal | subject to death
remorse | regret for wrongdoing
mortify | to subdue; to humiliate

Test Yourself

Define the following words.

1. mortuary _____
2. mortician _____
3. mortification _____
4. immortal _____
5. mortuous _____

Recognizing Words

Match the definitions in the right column with the words in the left column.

6. remorseful
7. moribund
8. mortally
9. immortality
10. immortalize

a. to make deathless
b. bothered by regret
c. fatally
d. deathlessness
e. dying

(Answers on page 180.)

Lesson 86

ROOT: MULTI, MULTUS
MEANING: much, many

Example
multiply
multiple
multivitamin

Meaning
to increase in number greatly
having more than one, many
containing several vitamins

Test Yourself
Define the following words.

1. multitudinous _____
2. multiplex _____
3. multipod _____
4. multiparous _____
5. multimillionaire _____

Recognizing Words

Match the definitions in the right column with the words in the left column.

6. multilingual
7. multitude
8. multistory
9. multiplier
10. multicolored

a. able to speak more than one language
b. having several stories
c. a number by which another number is multiplied
d. a great number
e. being of many colors

(Answers on page 180.)

Lesson 87

ROOT: NASC, NAT
MEANING: born

Example
natal
nativity
native

Meaning
having to do with birth
the process of birth
a member by right of birth

Test Yourself
Define the following words.

1. natural   _____
2. nativism   _____
3. innate   _____
4. nascent   _____
5. nationality   _____

Recognizing Words

Match the definitions in the right column with the words in the left column.

6. nationalism   a. born again
7. naturalize   b. birth
8. nascency   c. duty to homeland
9. natality   d. to make native or natural
10. renascence   e. birthrate

(Answers on page 180.)

Lesson 88

ROOT: NEUR
MEANING: nerve

Example
neural

neuralgia
neurology

Meaning
having to do with a nerve or the nervous system
acute pain along a nerve
area of medicine dealing with the nervous system

Test Yourself
Define the following words.

1. neurologist   _____
2. neurogenic   _____
3. neurosis   _____
4. neuroid   _____
5. neuritis   _____

Recognizing Words

Match the definitions in the right column with the words in the left column.

6. neuroleptic
7. neuropathic
8. neuron
9. neurography
10. neuroactive

a. a tranquilizer
b. description of the nervous system
c. nerve cell
d. suffering from a nerve disease
e. stimulating nerve tissue

(Answers on page 181.)

Lesson 89

ROOT: NOUNCE, NUNC
MEANING: declare, warn

Example
announce
pronounce
enunciate

Meaning
to declare publicly
to speak a word
to declare definitely; to articulate

Test Yourself

Define the following words.

1. denounce _____
2. renounce _____
3. annunciation _____
4. nuncio _____
5. announcer _____

Recognizing Words

Match the definitions in the right column with the words in the left column.

6. denunciation
7. nunciate
8. pronunciation
9. renunciation
10. pronouncement

a. a formal declaration of opinion
b. articulation
c. the process of revoking
d. messenger
e. a declaration of blame

(Answers on page 181.)

Lesson 90

ROOT: NOV
MEANING: new

Example
novel (adj.)
novelty
novice

Meaning
new
something new
beginner

Test Yourself

Define the following words.

1. renovate _____
2. nova _____
3. novacaine _____
4. innovation _____
5. novitiate _____

Recognizing Words

Match the definitions in the right column with the words in the left column.

6. novation
7. novator
8. novalike
9. nouveau riche
10. renovate

a. like a nova
b. substitution of a new legal obligation for an old one
c. one who renews
d. newly rich person
e. to introduce as new

(Answers on page 181.)

Lesson 91

ROOT: NUMBER, NUMER
MEANING: number

Example
numeral
numerable
numeration

Meaning
having to do with a number
the ability to be numbered
the process of counting

Test Yourself
Define the following words.

1. numerate _____
2. numerous _____
3. numeric _____
4. numerative _____
5. numberless _____

Recognizing Words
Match the definitions in the right column with the words in the left column.

6. numerator
7. enumerate
8. unnumbered
9. numerology
10. innumerable

a. not able to be counted
b. to count by ones
c. the study of the mystic qualities of numbers
d. upper number of a fraction
e. haven't been counted

(Answers on page 181.)

Lesson 92

ROOT: OPER, OPUS
MEANING: function, work

Example
cooperation
operate
operator

Meaning
working together
to work
one who works

Test Yourself

Define the following words.

1. opus _____
2. operatee _____
3. operation _____
4. operational _____
5. opuscule _____

Recognizing Words

Match the definitions in the right column with the words in the left column.

6. operose
7. operant
8. opera
9. cooperate
10. uncooperative

a. a dramatical, musical work
b. tedious
c. effective
d. unwilling to work together
e. to work together

(Answers on page 181.)

Lesson 93

ROOT: OSS, OSTEO
MEANING: bone

Example   **Meaning**
ossify   to make into bone
osteology   branch of anatomy that deals with bones
osteitis   inflammation of the bone

Test Yourself

Define the following words.

1. osteal _____
2. ossifrage _____
3. ossicle _____
4. osseous _____
5. ossuary _____

Recognizing Words

Match the definitions in the right column with the words in the left column.

6. ossification
7. osteopathy
8. osteoma
9. osteoblast
10. osteoplastic

a. relating to the replacement of bone by surgery
b. treatment of disease by means of manipulating the bones
c. process of bone production
d. a bone-forming cell
e. benign tumor made up of bone tissue

(Answers on page 182.)

Lesson 94

ROOT: PATER, PATR
MEANING: father

Example
paternal
patrician
patron

Meaning
derived from a father
person of high birth
a wealthy supporter

Test Yourself
Define the following words.

1. patronage _____
2. patronize _____
3. patriarch _____
4. patrimony _____
5. patricide _____

Recognizing Words

Match the definitions in the right column with the words in the left column.

6. expatriate
7. patriot
8. patrilineal
9. paternity
10. patronymic

a. relating to descent through the paternal line
b. fatherhood
c. exile
d. person true to his fatherland
e. father's name added to child's name

(Answers on page 182.)

Lesson 95

ROOT: PED, POD
MEANING: foot

Example   **Meaning**
pedal   lever worked by the foot; of the foot
quadruped   possessing four feet
pedestrian   walker

Test Yourself

Define the following words.

1. pediment _____
2. pedestal _____
3. impede _____
4. chiropodist _____
5. tripod _____

Recognizing Words

Match the definitions in the right column with the words in the left column.

6. bipod   a. possessing two feet
7. expedient   b. possessing a false foot
8. arthropod   c. literally "crane's foot"; the shape made by a genealogical chart
9. pseudopod   d. member of a group of invertebrates possessing jointed limbs
10. pedigree   e. designed for reaching a specific goal

(Answers on page 182.)

Lesson 96

ROOT: PEL, PULS
MEANING: drive, push, throw

Example | Meaning
compel — to drive (with force)
impel — to drive forward
dispel — to drive away

Test Yourself
Define the following words.

1. propel _____
2. repel _____
3. expel _____
4. pulse _____
5. impulsive _____

Recognizing Words

Match the definitions in the right column with the words in the left column.

6. propellant
7. repellant
8. propellor
9. appellate
10. appellation

a. something that drives something away
b. something that motivates
c. designation
d. revolving blades which cause motion of a vehicle
e. having power to review decisions of a lower court

(Answers on page 182.)

Lesson 97

ROOT: PEND, PENS
MEANING: hang, weigh, pay

Example **Meaning**
pendant   hanging ornament
append   to attach (something extra)

Test Yourself
Define the following words.

1. appendage _____
2. compendium _____
3. stipend   _____

Recognizing Words

Read the following paragraph and fill in each blank with the appropriate word. Definitions are in parentheses.

a. perpendicular (attached to another object at a right angle)
b. pendulous (hanging loosely)
c. suspend (to hang as though free except at one point)
d. spend (to pay out)
e. impending (hang threateningly)

If you ____4____ money on that hanging planter, you'll be wasting your money. First, the design is too severe and geometrical. Second, the decor of the room doesn't lend itself to ____5____ ornaments because the rest of the furnishings are horizontal in design. Besides, the spot you've chosen is directly over my desk and I will sit underneath the planter with a sense of ____6____ doom. If you insist on buying the ____7____ planter, I'll have to ask you to ____8____ it from the ceiling in a place which is not directly over my head.

(Answers on page 182.)

Lesson 98

ROOT: PHIL, PHILA, PHILE, PHILO
MEANING: love

Example
philosophy
philology
philanthropy

Meaning
pursuit of wisdom
the study of literature
love of fellow man

Test Yourself

Define the following words.

1. philter _____
2. philander _____
3. philogyny _____
4. philhellene _____
5. philogeant _____

Recognizing Words

Match the definitions in the right column with the words in the left column.

6. Philharmonic
7. philosopher
8. anglophilia
9. philomath
10. philanderer

a. admirer of England and all English things
b. a symphony orchestra
c. lover of wisdom
d. male who makes love to many women with no intention of marriage
e. lover of learning

(Answers on page 183.)

Lesson 99

ROOT: PHOTO, PHOS
MEANING: light

Example
photography

photometer
photosensitive

Meaning
process of producing images on a sensitized surface by the action of light
a device used to measure light
sensitive to light

Test Yourself
Define the following words.

1. telephoto _____
2. photosynthesis _____
3. phototropic _____
4. phosphorous _____
5. phosphate _____

Recognizing Words
Match the definitions in the right column with the words in the left column.

6. photomicrograph
7. photomural
8. photon
9. photoplay
10. photocopy

a. photographic reproduction of printed or written material
b. motion picture; movie
c. a unit of radiant energy
d. photographic display of a magnified object
e. an enlarged photograph

(Answers on page 183.)

Lesson 100

ROOT: PICT, PICTO
MEANING: paint

Example
picture

pictorial

Meaning
a representation made by means of a photograph, drawing, painting

having to do with or consisting of pictures

Test Yourself

Define the following words.

1. pictograph _____
2. pictoradiogram _____
3. picturer _____
4. picturize _____
5. picturesqueness _____

Recognizing Words

Match the definitions in the right column with the words in the left column.

6. depict
7. depiction
8. picturedrome
9. pictography
10. depiction

a. the act of representing
b. a moving-picture theatre
c. to portray; describe
d. picture writing
e. a portrayal

(Answers on page 183.)

Lesson 101

                    ROOT: PLAC, PLAIS
                    MEANING: please

Example
placid
complacent
placate

Meaning
calm, undisturbed
pleased with oneself
to please by giving concessions

Test Yourself
Define the following words.

1. placebo
2. implacable
3. placater
4. placidness
5. placation

Recognizing Words

Match the definitions in the right column with the words in the left column.

6. complaisance   a. state of being difficult to please
7. complaisantly   b. obligingly
8. placatory   c. soothing
9. placability   d. tractability
10. implacability   e. affability

(Answers on page 183.)

Lesson 102

ROOT: PLU, PLUR, PLUS
MEANING: more

Example   **Meaning**

plural   a word form used to denote more than one

plus   an added quantity

surplus   an excess

Test Yourself

Define the following words.

1. pluralize
2. pluralization
3. plurality
4. plurisyllable
5. plurinomial

Recognizing Words

Match the definitions in the right column with the words in the left column.

6. plurilingual
7. plurilateral
8. pluperfect
9. nonplus
10. plussage

a. amount over and above another
b. the past perfect tense
c. having more than one side
d. a state of bafflement
e. having more than one language

(Answers on page 183.)

Lesson 103

ROOT: PNEUM, PNEUMON, PNE
MEANING: breath, air

Example
pneumatic
pneumonia
pneumatology

Meaning
having to do with the using of air
inflammation of the lungs
study of spiritual beings or phenomena

Test Yourself
Define the following words.

1. pneumonic _____

2. pneumotropic _____

Recognizing Words

Match the definitions in the right column with the words in the left column.

3. pneumectomy   a. device used to measure exerted force of lungs while breathing

4. pneumoconiosis   b. branch of physics dealing with air and gases

5. pneumatometer   c. removal of a lung or part of a lung

6. pneumatogram   d. disease of the lungs caused by dust

7. pneumatics   e. printed display which traces respiratory movements

(Answers on page 184.)

Lesson 104

ROOT: PON, POS, POSE
MEANING: place, put, position

Example
component
proposition
opponent

Meaning
ingredient
something offered for consideration
adversary; one positioned against you

Test Yourself
Define the following words.

1. proponent _____
2. postpone _____
3. deponent _____
4. suppose _____
5. repository _____

Recognizing Words

Match the definitions in the right column with the words in the left column.

6. supposition
7. posit
8. compost
9. deposit
10. interpose

a. to assume the existence of
b. to place
c. to place between
d. fertilizing material consisting mainly of organic material
e. hypothesis

(Answers on page 184.)

Lesson 105

ROOT: POPUL
MEANING: people

Example
populace
popular
popularity

Meaning
the people
having to do with the people
quality of being loved by the people

Test Yourself

Define the following words.

1. depopulate _____
2. unpopular _____
3. populicide _____
4. populism _____
5. population _____

Recognizing Words

Match the definitions in the right column with the words in the left column.

6. depopulator
7. populate
8. popularize
9. populous
10. popularism

a. saturated with inhabitants
b. to cater to people's taste
c. something which causes a population's decrease
d. democratic movement
e. to furnish with people

(Answers on page 184.)

Lesson 106

ROOT: PORT
MEANING: carry

Example
porter
portable
portage

Meaning
one who carries
moveable
a route for the carrying of boats and goods from one body of water to another

Test Yourself

Define the following words.

1. reporter _____
2. comport _____
3. disport _____
4. export _____
5. import _____

Recognizing Words

Match the definitions in the right column with the words in the left column.

6. purport
7. transport
8. portfolio
9. deportment
10. support

a. implied meaning
b. behavior
c. to carry across
d. to hold up, or carry
e. a file which can be carried

(Answers on page 184.)

Lesson 107

ROOT: PORTION
MEANING: share, part

Example
portion (n.)
disproportion

Meaning
part, share
not suitable after comparison

Test Yourself

Define the following words.

1. portion (v.) _____

2. proportional _____

3. disproportionate _____

Recognizing Words

Read the following paragraph and fill in each blank with the correct word. Definitions are in parentheses.

a. apportionable (having the qualities required to be given out as a share)
b. portionable (having the qualities required to be divided)
c. portionless (without shares or parts)
d. portioner (divider)
e. apportion (the act of sharing out or portioning)

   The man was expected to act as the official ____4____ of the estate. His decision as to how the estate was to be made ____5____ was to be final. Some of the estate's most valuable items did not appear to be ____6____. They seemed to be in a form that left them ____7____. How was he going to decide to ____8____ the painting over the fireplace without selling it for much less than it was worth as a delight to the eyes.

(Answers on page 184.)

Lesson 108

ROOT: POTEN, POTES, POSSE
MEANING: power

Example
potent
possible
impotent

Meaning
powerful, strong, capable
capable of being
incapable, weak, lacking power

Test Yourself

Define the following words.

1. potence _____
2. potestative _____
3. possess _____
4. potentiality _____
5. potentiate _____

Recognizing Words

Read the following paragraph and fill in each blank with the correct word. Definitions are in parentheses.

a. impossible (incapable of being, hopeless)
b. positive (affirmative)
c. possibility (condition of being possible)
d. possessor (owner)
e. possee (group of assistants)

It was totally ____6____ for the sherriff's ____7____ to determine which man was the ____8____ of the illegal handgun. We hope that lab tests will provide ____9____ evidence so that we can enjoy the ____10____ of a clean conviction.

(Answers on page 185.)

Lesson 109

ROOT: PRIM, PRIN
MEANING: first

Example
prime
primal
primacy

Meaning
the earliest stage; first
original
the first (as in rank or office)

Test Yourself
Define the following words.

1. primeval   _____
2. primer   _____
3. primordial _____
4. primogeniture _____
5. primate   _____

Recognizing Words

Match the definitions in the right column with the words in the left column.

6. primitive
7. primatial
8. principal
9. primogenitor
10. prime (adj.)

a. having position of first rank
b. earliest traceable ancestor
c. first, best, most valuable
d. of the first times or earliest times
e. most important

(Answers on page 185.)

Lesson 110

ROOT: PUNG, PUNCT
MEANING: to prick, to point

Example
punctuate
pungent
punctiform

Meaning
to mark a sentence with standardized signals
to the point; caustic
possessing the shape of a dot

Test Yourself
Define the following words.

1. punctilio _____
2. punctuator _____
3. punctuation _____
4. compunction _____
5. punctual _____

Recognizing Words
Match the definitions in the right column with the words in the left column.

6. puncture
7. punctographic
8. acupuncture
9. punctate
10. punctilious

a. writing done using points as symbols; Braille
b. to produce a wound which resembles a dot on the skin
c. Chinese practice of puncturing the body to cure disease
d. most exact
e. occurring in dots or points

(Answers on page 185.)

Lesson 111

ROOT: PUT, PUTE
MEANING: correct, prune

Example　　**Meaning**
putative　　commonly supposed
compute　　to count

Test Yourself

Define the following words.

1. impute　　_____
2. deputy　　_____
3. amputate　　_____
4. reputation　　_____
5. computation　　_____

Recognizing Words

Match the definitions in the right column with the words in the left column.

6. amputation
7. deputation
8. repute
9. disputation
10. computer

a. the character ascribed to one by others
b. debate
c. the act of cutting off
d. one that computes; an electronic device for storing, retrieving, and processing data
e. the act of making one responsible for another or others

(Answers on page 185.)

Lesson 112

ROOT: RECT, RECTI
MEANING: right, straight, rule

Example
rectangle
rectilinear
direct

Meaning
right-angled parallelogram
forming a straight line
to show the right way

Test Yourself
Define the following words.

1. rector _____
2. rectitude _____
3. directory _____
4. reckoning _____
5. rectify _____

Recognizing Words

Match the definitions in the right column with the words in the left column.

6. direction   a. an order of the way to proceed
7. directly   b. process of showing the right way
8. directive   c. calculator
9. indirect   d. not in a straight line
10. reckoner   e. without delay

(Answers on page 185.)

Lesson 113

ROOT: RID, RIS
MEANING: laugh

Example
deride
ridiculous
derision

Meaning
to laugh at scornfully
laughable
scornful laughing

Test Yourself
Define the following words.

1. risible   _____
2. riant   _____
3. derisive   _____
4. ridicule (v.) _____
5. risibility   _____

Recognizing Words

Match the definitions in the right column with the words in the left column.

6. derisively
7. ridiculousness
8. riantly
9. ridiculer
10. ridibund

a. having a tendency to laughter
b. scornfully, mockingly
c. one who mocks
d. a state of being laughable
e. laughingly

(Answers on page 186.)

Lesson 114

ROOT: SANG, SANGUI
MEANING: blood

Example
sanguine (adj.)
consanguinity
sanguinary

Meaning
red; blood-like; confident
possessing common relatives
bloodthirsty

Test Yourself

Define the following words.

1. sanguine (n) _____
2. saguinity _____
3. sanguinarily _____
4. sanguineless _____
5. sanguineous _____

Recognizing Words

Match the definitions in the right column with the words in the left column.

6. sanguimotor
7. sanguify
8. sangfroid
9. sanguinolent
10. sanguinaceous

a. having to do with the circulation of the blood
b. to make blood
c. full-blooded
d. self-possession under strain
e. containing blood

(Answers on page 186.)

Lesson 115

ROOT: SCOP
MEANING: see, look

Example
telescope
microscope

Meaning
instrument for seeing distant objects
instrument for seeing minute objects

Test Yourself

Define the following words.

1. kaleidoscope _____
2. gyroscope   _____
3. helioscope   _____
4. periscopic   _____
5. radioscope   _____

Recognizing Words

Match the definitions in the right column with the words in the left column.

6. flouroscope
7. spectroscope
8. seismoscope
9. cystoscope
10. baroscope

a. instrument used to record movement of the earth's crust
b. instrument used to view the interior of the human body
c. instrument used to view the spectrum of the sun
d. instrument used to reveal changes in atmospheric pressure
e. instrument for the visual examination of the bladder

(Answers on page 186.)

Lesson 116

ROOT: SIGN, SIGNI
MEANING: mark, sign

Example
sign
signal

significance

Meaning
a mark; symbol
a symbol or mark agreed upon as the start of some action
meaning; suggestiveness

Test Yourself

Define the following words.

1. assignation _____
2. consign _____
3. designate _____
4. design _____
5. resign _____

Recognizing Words

Match the definitions in the right column with the words in the left column.

6. designation
7. resignation
8. insignia

9. assignment
10. signaler

a. distinguishing mark
b. the act of formally quitting
c. communicator utilizing symbols or signs
d. symbol; name; title
e. task

(Answers on page 186.)

Lesson 117

ROOT: SILIC
MEANING: flint

Example **Meaning**
silicon   nonmetallic element naturally found in geologic formations throughout the world
silica   silicon dioxide

Test Yourself

Define the following words.

1. silicosis _____
2. siliceous _____
3. silicic _____

Recognizing Words

Match the definitions in the right column with the words in the left column.

4. silicate
5. silicify
6. silicification
7. siliciferous
8. silicam

a. a silicon-derived compound
b. to impregnate with silica
c. uniting with, containing, or producing silica
d. the act of filling with silica
e. a salt derived from a silicic acid

(Answers on page 186.)

Lesson 118

ROOT: SIMIL, SIMUL
MEANING: like, same

Example
similar
simile

assimilate

Meaning
like, same
a comparison made using the words like or as
to make or become like something

Test Yourself

Define the following words.

1. simulate _____
2. verisimilitude _____
3. simultaneous _____
4. simulacrum _____
5. similarity _____

Recognizing Words

Match the definitions in the right column with the words in the left column.

6. simulator
7. dissimilar
8. similative
9. similitude
10. simulcast

a. likeness, resemblance
b. having a tendency to create resemblances
c. to broadcast simultaneously
d. one who creates resemblances
e. having no resemblance

(Answers on page 187.)

Lesson 119

ROOT: SIST, STA, STET, STIT
MEANING: stand

Example **Meaning**
assist   to help
consist   to be composed of
insist   to take a resolute stand

Test Yourself
Define the following words.

1. subsist   _____
2. existence   _____
3. status   _____
4. resist   _____
5. persist   _____

Recognizing Words

Match the definitions in the right column with the words in the left column.

6. exist   a. faithful; steadfast
7. stanchion   b. upright post
8. constant   c. to stand in the place of another
9. substitute   d. to be
10. obstinate   e. stubborn

(Answers on page 187.)

Lesson 120

ROOT: SOPH
MEANING: wisdom

Example
sophism
sophistry
sophomore

Meaning
deceptively reasonable argument
deceptive logic
student in his/her second high school year

Test Yourself
Define the following words.

1. philosopher _____
2. sophist _____
3. sophisticated _____
4. sophiology _____
5. sophical _____

Recognizing Words
Match the definitions in the right column with the words in the left column.

6. sophomoric
7. sophistication
8. sophisticator
9. philosophism
10. unsophisticate

a. falsification
b. falsifier
c. one who is not worldly
d. urbanity
e. immature

(Answers on page 187.)

Lesson 121

ROOT: SPEC, SPIC
MEANING: behold, look, see, observe

Example
specimen
specter
retrospect

Meaning
a sample of a certain kind or thing
ghost
a looking backward

Test Yourself
Define the following words.

1. introspection _____
2. aspect _____
3. circumspect _____
4. perspicacity _____
5. inspect _____

Recognizing Words

Match the definitions in the right column with the words in the left column.

6. spectator   a. fear of ghosts
7. spectral   b. observer
8. spectrum   c. easily understood
9. perspicuous   d. ghost-like
10. spectrophobia   e. continuous sequence or range

(Answers on page 187.)

Lesson 122

ROOT: SPHER
MEANING: ball, sphere

Example
sphere
spherical
spherics

Meaning
ball, globe, planet
having to do with a sphere
details of the science of spheres

Test Yourself

Define the following words.

1. sphericity _____
2. troposphere _____
3. photosphere _____
4. geosphere _____
5. lithosphere _____

Recognizing Words

Match the definitions in the right column with the words in the left column.

6. hemisphere
7. biosphere
8. spheroid
9. hydrosphere
10. stratosphere

a. the water and vapor in the atmosphere
b. half of a sphere
c. the area of a sphere containing living organisms
d. upper portion of earth's atmosphere
e. a solid, geometrical figure

(Answers on page 187.)

Lesson 123

ROOT: SPOND, SPONS
MEANING: answer, pledge

Example	Meaning
respond	answer, reply
sponsor (n)	one who takes responsibility for someone else
correspond	to be in agreement; communicate by letter

Test Yourself

Define the following words.

1. sponsor (v.) _____
2. responsible _____
3. correspondence _____
4. responder _____
5. sponsorial _____

Recognizing Words

Match the definitions in the right column with the words in the left column.

6. responsibility
7. responsive
8. sponsorship
9. correspondent
10. irresponsible

a. something for which one is answerable
b. not capable of answering for some duties
c. letter writer
d. quick to answer
e. the state of acting as a sponsor

(Answers on page 188.)

Lesson 124

ROOT: STRU, STRUCT
MEANING: build

Example
instrument
construct

Meaning
tool; device used to do work or build
build; make

Test Yourself

Define the following words.

1. destruction _____
2. superstructure _____
3. instruct _____
4. obstruct _____
5. structural _____

Recognizing Words

Read the following paragraph and fill in the blanks with the correct word. Definitions are in parentheses.

a. obstruction (a blockage)
b. destruct (to destroy; ruin)
c. reconstruct (to build again)
d. instructions (lessons; directions)
e. misconstrue (to interpret incorrectly)

   Please don't ____6____ my written ____7____. Your inability to understand will prove to be an ____8____ to the entire project. If we fall behind our deadline, we'll have to ____9____ all parts of the project we've worked so hard to complete. Without our hard work the project could just self-____10____.

(Answers on page 188.)

Lesson 125

ROOT: SUM, SUMPT
MEANING: take

Example   **Meaning**
assumption   something taken for granted
resume   to take up or assume again

Test Yourself

Define the following words.

1. presume   _____
2. consume   _____
3. sumptuosity _____
4. presumptive _____
5. resumption _____

Recognizing Words

Read the following paragraph and fill in each blank with the correct word. Definitions are in parentheses.

a. sumptous (luxurious; lavish)
b. consumptive (destructive; wasteful; used up)
c. consumers (users)
d. consumable (possessing the ability to be eaten, taken in or used)
e. consumption (the act of eating up or using up)

Sometimes I wonder why our society is so incredibly ____6____. We seem to be a world leader when it comes to ____7____ of our world's natural resources. Many of our citizens are blatant ____8____, and their lifestyles are embarrassingly ____9____. I'm beginning to worry about our ____10____ resources.

(Answers on page 188.)

Lesson 126

ROOT: TACT, TAG, TANG, TIG
MEANING: touch

Example
intangible
tacky
contact

Meaning
incapable of being touched
sticky to the touch
touch

Test Yourself

Define the following words.

1. tact _____
2. tangible _____
3. contamination _____
4. contiguous _____
5. tangled _____

Recognizing Words

Match the definitions in the right column with the words in the left column.

6. contagious
7. tactile
8. intact
9. tactual
10. tangent

a. perceptible through the sense of touch
b. not altered
c. communicable by touch
d. a line which touches the surface of a curve at one point
e. having to do with tact or knowing the right behavior

(Answers on page 188.)

Lesson 127

ROOT: TAIN, TEN, TIN
MEANING: hold

Example
contain
abstain
continent (adj)
tenacious

Meaning
to hold; have within
to restrain oneself; leave off
possessing self-restraint
holding fast

Test Yourself

Define the following words.

1. container _____
2. detain _____
3. attain _____
4. entertain _____
5. obtain _____

Recognizing Words

Match the definitions in the right column with the words in the left column.

6. pertain
7. retain
8. tenant
9. tenet
10. continue

a. one who rents or leases (as a house)
b. to belong to as a part or quality
c. to hold in possession
d. principles held in common by the majority
e. to hold in a place or condition

(Answers on page 188.)

Lesson 128

ROOT: TECHN
MEANING: skill, art

Example
technical

technician

Meaning
having to do with special knowledge of a mechanical or a scientific object

a person skilled in the area of a specific mechanical or scientific subject

Test Yourself

Define the following words.

1. technics _____
2. technicalist _____
3. pyrotechnics _____
4. technocracy _____
5. technology _____

Recognizing Words

Match the definitions in the right column with the words in the left column.

6. technologist
7. technonomy
8. techniphone
9. hydrotechny
10. technocrat

a. the use of water for industrial processes
b. expert in technology
c. a person working in industrial arts or applied science
d. laws of the science of industrial arts
e. a non-functioning keyboard for typing practice

(Answers on page 189.)

Lesson 129

ROOT: TEM, TEMPO, TEMPOR
MEANING: time

Example
temporary
temporal
contemporary

Meaning
impermanent, passing
of, relating to, or limited by time
occurring or existing at the same time

Test Yourself

Define the following words.

1. extemporaneous _____
2. tempo _____
3. temporarily _____
4. temporize _____

Recognizing Words

Match the definitions in the right column with the words in the left column.

5. extemporaneously
6. pro tem
7. temporariness
8. temporization

9. extempore

a. for the time being
b. impromptu
c. impermanence
d. the act of complying with the time or circumstance
e. on the spur of the moment; unprepared

(Answers on page 189.)

Lesson 130

ROOT: TEND, TENS, TENT
MEANING: stretch, strain

Example / Meaning
intend — to plan; to have in mind for an aim
pretend — to profess; to lay claim
contend — to strive against opposition

Test Yourself
Define the following words.

1. distend _____
2. superintend _____
3. tension _____
4. intent _____
5. ostensible _____

Recognizing Words
Match the definitions in the right column with the words in the left column.

6. intense
7. tensile
8. extensive
9. extenuate
10. portentious

a. having to do with the strength against tension
b. to treat as of less importance than is generally apparent
c. straining to the maximum
d. self-consciously weighty or important
e. far-reaching

(Answers on page 189.)

Lesson 131

ROOT: TEST
MEANING: bear witness

Example
attest
protest
testament

Meaning
to certify as true
to object strongly
evidence; an act by which a person determines the dividing of his personal property after his death

Test Yourself

Define the following words.

1. testify
2. testimonial
3. contest
4. detest
5. testation

Recognizing Words

Match the definitions in the right column with the words in the left column.

6. testator
7. intestate
8. contestable
9. testification
10. protester

a. challengeable
b. one who objects strongly
c. act of bearing witness
d. author of a will
e. having no will at the time of death

(Answers on page 189.)

Lesson 132

ROOT: THE, THEO
MEANING: god

Example | **Meaning**
theology | study of God and religious truth; divinity
theologist | student of religion
theism | belief in existence of a god or gods

Test Yourself

Define the following words.

1. monotheism _____
2. theocracy   _____
3. pantheism   _____
4. atheism   _____
5. apotheosis _____

Recognizing Words

Match the definitions in the right column with the words in the left column.

6. atheist
7. theogony
8. theocratic
9. theocrat
10. theogamy

a. a follower of theocracy
b. the origin of the gods or an account of this
c. marriage of gods
d. having to do with a government ruled by divine guidance
e. one denying the existence of god

(Answers on page 189.)

Lesson 133

ROOT: TRACT, TRĂH
MEANING: draw, pull

Example
attract
contract (v)

Meaning
to draw towards oneself
to draw together, shrink

Test Yourself

Define the following words.

1. attraction _____
2. abstract (v) _____
3. detract _____
4. protract _____

Recognizing Words

Read the following paragraph and fill in each blank with the correct word. Definitions are in parentheses.

a. detractors (persons who disparage another's reputation)
b. retraction (withdrawal)
c. abstract (speech, statement)
d. contract (n) (agreement)
e. tractable (easily managed)

I've got to write an ____5____ which summarizes the lawsuit over the disputed ____6____. On top of this, my afternoon has to be spent talking the local newspaper into printing a ____7____ of their story questioning our candidate's credibility. The editors are strong-willed, not easily ____8____. Our candidate's ____9____ are having a field day exploiting this story against us.

(Answers on page 190.)

Lesson 134

ROOT: TRIB
MEANING: pay, bestow

Example — **Meaning**
tribute — a gift, service, or speech showing respect
distribute — to divide among many
contribute — to supply or furnish a share

Test Yourself

Define the following words.

1. distribution _____
2. contribution _____
3. attribution _____
4. redistribute _____
5. retribution _____

Recognizing Words

Match the definitions in the right column with the words in the left column.

6. contributional
7. distributor
8. attribute (n.)
9. tributary
10. attributive

a. a quality
b. having to do with gifts given as aid or to help
c. pertaining to a quality
d. paying tribute; flowing into a larger stream
e. person responsible for dividing among many

(Answers on page 190.)

Lesson 135

ROOT: TU
MEANING: teach, guard

Example
tutor
intuent
intuitive

Meaning
teacher
having knowledge by insight
possessing the quality of insight

Test Yourself
Define the following words.

1. tuition   _____
2. tutorial   _____
3. intuition   _____
4. intuitivism   _____
5. intuitionist   _____

Recognizing Words
Match the definitions in the right column with the words in the left column.

6. tuitional
7. tutorly
8. tutorage
9. tutoriate
10. intuit

a. having to do with a teacher
b. to know by insight
c. a faculty consisting of teachers
d. the office of being a tutor
e. having to do with teaching or the payment for it

(Answers on page 190.)

Lesson 136

ROOT: UNI
MEANING: one

Example
unit
unify

Meaning
the least whole number; one
to make into a unit; cause a group to act as one

Test Yourself
Define the following words.

1. uniform (adj.) _____
2. unicycle _____
3. unicorn _____
4. unicameral _____
5. unicellular _____

Recognizing Words
Match the definitions in the right column with the words in the left column.

6. unification
7. unilateral
8. union
9. universe
10. unique

a. an act or instance of combining two or more into a unit
b. every conceivable thing or idea viewed as a system or whole
c. the act or process of making something into a unit
d. one of a kind
e. of, having, affecting, or done by one side only

(Answers on page 190.)

Lesson 137

ROOT: VAC
MEANING: empty

Example
vacuum
vacant
vacuole

Meaning
space entirely empty of matter
empty
empty space within a cell

Test Yourself
Define the following words.

1. vacation _____
2. evacuant _____
3. vacancy _____
4. vacate _____
5. vacuity _____

Recognizing Words
Match the definitions in the right column with the words in the left column.

6. vacationist
7. vacual
8. vacuous

9. evacuee
10. evacuation

a. a person who has been taken away from a dangerous area
b. having to do with a vacuum
c. the act of leaving a dangerous area
d. totally void of thought
e. a person on holiday

(Answers on page 190.)

Lesson 138

ROOT: VAL
MEANING: to be strong

Example   **Meaning**
value   worth
valid   sound legally; correct

Test Yourself

Define the following words.

1. prevalent   _____

2. valiant   _____

3. equivalent   _____

4. valediction   _____

Recognizing Words

Read the following paragraph and fill in each blank with the correct word. Definitions are in parentheses.

a. valedictorian (student who delivers the farewell speech)
b. validity (soundness; logic)
c. validate (to make valid, declare legal)
d. valor (value, worth, strength)
e. evaluate (to find the value of)

     It takes a certain amount of ____5____ to get up in front of the entire student body to deliver a farewell graduation speech. The ____6____ must be admired for bravery when performing this task. When a school is asked to ____7____ a student's academic achievements, the school should also recognize, praise, and ____8____ instances of a student's nonacademic attainments. There is ____9____ in trying to develop well-rounded citizens within our school system.

(Answers on page 191.)

Lesson 139

ROOT: VEN
MEANING: come

Example
convene
contravene
revenue

Meaning
to assemble
to act contrary to
investment income

Test Yourself

Define the following words.

1. intervene _____
2. supervene _____
3. venture (n.) _____
4. advent _____
5. circumvent _____

Recognizing Words

Match the definitions in the right column with the words in the left column.

6. invent
7. prevent
8. preventative
9. adventitious
10. intervention

a. to keep from happening
b. having to do with hindering
c. to devise
d. a coming between; an interruption
e. accidental, incidental

(Answers on page 191.)

Lesson 140

ROOT: VER
MEANING: true, genuine

Example | Meaning
verity — reality, truth
verify — to establish the truth of
veracious — truthful

Test Yourself
Define the following words.

1. very
2. verisimilitude
3. aver
4. verdict
5. verily

Recognizing Words

Match the definitions in the right column with the words in the left column.

6. verification
7. verifier
8. verifiable
9. verificate
10. veracity

a. possessing the capability of establishing the truth
b. the act of establishing the truth
c. accuracy; truth
d. to confirm
e. one who establishes the truth

(Answers on page 191.)

Lesson 141

ROOT: VERS, VERT
MEANING: turn

Example   Meaning
versatile   turning with ease from one thing or position to another
version   a personal account of something
aversion   something decidedly disliked

Test Yourself
Define the following words.

1. subversion   _____
2. irreversible   _____
3. vertex   _____
4. convert (v)   _____

Recognizing Words
Read the following paragraph and fill in each blank with the correct word. Definitions are in parentheses.

a. vertical (upright; overhead)
b. versus (against)
c. verse (poem)
d. adversary (foe; opponent)
e. reverse (opposite to a previous or normal condition)

    Once, in a book of poetry, I read a ____5____ about a hero and an ____6____. The hero charged with his sword held up over his head in a ____7____ position. His opponent charged past him, stopped, and charged again from the ____8____ side of the field of battle. The hero, tragically, was killed. So ended the poem of the hero ____9____ the villain.

(Answers on page 191.)

Lesson 142

ROOT: VEST
MEANING: clothe, to dress

Example
vest (n.)
vestee
vesture

Meaning
an article of clothing
a small, jacket-like piece of clothing
clothing

Test Yourself

Define the following words.

1. vestment _____
2. vestural _____
3. invest _____

Recognizing Words

Match the definitions in the right column with the words in the left column.

4. investor
5. vestiary
6. investiture
7. travesty
8. investment

a. pertaining to garments
b. money spent with hopes of future profit
c. a parody
d. the ceremony of presenting the robes of office
e. one who spends money with hopes that the purchases will bring profits

(Answers on page 191.)

Lesson 143

ROOT: VIC
MEANING: change, substitute, deputy

Example	Meaning
vicarious	taking the place of another
vicar	assistant capable of being a substitute; a clergyman
vicarage	home of a vicar

Test Yourself

Define the following words.

1. vicarly _____
2. vicissitude _____
3. vicissitous _____
4. vicissitudinous _____
5. vicarial _____

Recognizing Words

Match the definitions in the right column with the words in the left column.

6. vicariate (v.)
7. vicariousness
8. vicarate
9. vicarship
10. vicariously

a. the state of taking another's place or duty
b. the office or duties of vicar
c. substituting for another
d. to assume the duties of another
e. authority of a vicar

(Answers on page 192.)

Lesson 144

ROOT: VICT, VINE
MEANING: vanquish, conquer

Example   **Meaning**
victor   winner; conqueror
convict   to prove guilty
evict   to throw out

Test Yourself

Define the following words.

1. victory _____
2. conviction _____
3. eviction _____
4. convince _____
5. invincible _____

Recognizing Words

Match the definitions in the right column with the words in the left column.

6. evince
7. victorious
8. victimize
9. victim
10. invincibly

a. use as a sacrifice
b. in the manner of one who cannot be defeated
c. a person who is conquered
d. show; reveal
e. triumphant

(Answers on page 192.)

Lesson 145

ROOT: VID, VIS
MEANING: see

Example
visible
visor
visual

Meaning
capable of being seen
projecting front portion of a hat
having to do with or used in sight; perceived by seeing

Test Yourself

Define the following words.

1. vision   _____
2. advise   _____
3. visionary   _____
4. evident   _____
5. invidious   _____

Recognizing Words

Match the definitions in the right column with the words in the left column.

6. evidence   a. to make, invent or arrange on the spur of the moment
7. provident   b. making provision for the future
8. supervise   c. to have a mental picture of
9. improvise   d. oversee
10. envisage   e. an outward sign; proof

(Answers on page 192.)

Lesson 146

ROOT: VITA, VIV, VIVI
MEANING: life

Example   **Meaning**
vivid   intense; full of life
revive   to return or restore to life
survive   to remain alive

Test Yourself

Define the following words.

1. vitality _____
2. vital _____
3. survival _____
4. revival _____
5. vivacious _____

Recognizing Words

Match the definitions in the right column with the words in the left column.

6. vivisection   a. enjoying companionship
7. convivial   b. producing live young as opposed to egg-laying
8. viviparous   c. the cutting of or operation on a living animal
9. vitalize   d. to cut something living
10. vivisect   e. to impart life or vigor to

(Answers on page 192.)

Lesson 147

ROOT: VOC, VOK
MEANING: call, word

Example
vocal
advocation

Meaning
uttered by the voice
the act of arguing or pleading for another's cause

Test Yourself

Define the following words.

1. vouchsafe _____
2. vociferous _____
3. advocate (n.) _____
4. vocable (n.) _____
5. convoke _____

Recognizing Words

Read the following paragraph and fill in each blank with the correct word. Definitions are in parentheses.

a. evoke (to call forth)
b. vocation (chosen occupation)
c. revoke (to annul by recalling or taking back)
d. invoke (to make an earnest request for)

   I have a daughter aspiring to a ____6____ as a vocalist who is a member of the chorus in your opera company. Her voice is enough to ____7____ the angels from heaven. I ____8____ you to listen to her, judge her talent, and I'm sure you'll not decide to ____9____ her contract which is up for renewal.

(Answers on page 192.)

Lesson 148

ROOT: VOLCAN, VULCAN
MEANING: fire

Example | **Meaning**
Vulcan | Roman god of fire
volcano | birth of a mountain by eruption of a weak point in the earth's crust
volcanic | characteristic of a volcano

Test Yourself
Define the following words.

1. volcanology _____
2. volcanism _____
3. vulcanization _____

Recognizing Words

Match the definitions in the right column with the words in the left column.

4. volcanologist
5. volcanist

6. volcanite
7. vulcanian

8. volcanize

a. rare rock of volcanic origin
b. an expert in the area of volcanic phenomena
c. to suffer volcanic heat
d. student of volcanic eruptions
e. having to do with work done with iron and other metals

(Answers on page 193.)

PUZZLES

Directions: Crossword Puzzles are an enjoyable way to develop your vocabulary. Try these puzzles and check your answers at the back of the book. Don't be afraid to look up the words you don't know in a dictionary.

Puzzle 1

ACROSS

1. Aquatic mammal
5. Snide insult
9. Dressing gowns
14. Confine
15. Toward shelter
16. Dodge
17. Exchange premium
18. Frost
19. Weak
20. Unit of resistance
21. Oleoresin
23. —— Vegas
24. Builds
28. Chinese dynasty
30. Ocean vessel
33. Remove
37. Grooved
41. Carnegie et al.
42. Pursue
43. Thin cracker
45. Smack
46. Modify
48. Essential
50. Elapses
52. Hindu queen
53. Follow: sl.
55. Examined
59. Time zone: abbr.
62. Stream
65. Film name
66. Floating
68. Suitcase
70. Individualist: sl.
71. Streetshow
72. Pilaster
73. Tree
74. Frets: sl.
75. Unpleasant glance
76. Makes lace

DOWN

1. Intimidate
2. Wishful
3. Lithe
4. Man's name
5. Exclamation
6. Medicinal herb
7. —— estate
8. Headwear
9. Purified
10. Eggs
11. Security bond
12. Girl's name
13. Collector's goals
22. Insane
25. Dispute
26. Metal
27. Lots: colloq.
29. Tumblers
31. Ardor
32. Allude
34. She: Italian
35. Shred
36. Sight
37. Fellow
38. Kind of hoop
39. Insects
40. Ten: pref.
44. Budget item
47. Attains
49. Observe
51. Title for Olivier
54. Lawful
56. Girl's name
57. Occurrence
58. Is courageous
59. Head parts
60. Clout
61. Waste allowance
63. Sea eagle
64. Elanet
67. Hem
69. —— for the course
70. Elect

(Answers on page 194.)

Puzzle 2

ACROSS

1. Docile
5. Musty
10. Small measure
14. Wild goat
15. Moses' brother
16. Irritate: colloq.
17. Decree
18. Counts calories
19. Roman road
20. Word in F.B.I.
22. Come up for air
24. Short letters
26. Consume
27. Belief
30. Payable
32. Award
36. Some entrees
38. Milling crowd
40. Distribute
41. Chicken product
42. Droop
44. Bite
46. Farm animal
47. Vend
49. Humorist
51. City in Switzerland
53. Trample
55. Betel, e.g.
57. Artist's stand
58. Unit of resistance
60. Scorched
62. Snarls
66. Summaries
70. Central American tree
71. Cognizant
73. Enthuse
74. Charity
75. Jury
76. Celebes ox
77. Encounter
78. Small fights
79. Nasty look

DOWN

1. Petty fight
2. Man's nickname
3. Western lake
4. Lengthen
5. Egyptian president
6. Followed: sl.
7. Exist
8. —— wife
9. Result
10. Wandered aimlessly
11. Girl's name
12. Actor Guinness
13. Simple
21. Origins
23. Male sheep
25. Total
27. Peak
28. Man's name
29. Bird of prey
31. Time period
33. Sedates
34. Active
35. Within the law
37. Cutting tool
39. Huge
43. —— rummy
45. Hammer parts
48. Most out-sized
50. Place for a bath
52. —— gas
54. Eastern state: abbr.
56. Gun tower
59. Jumps
61. Lively dances
62. Group of players
63. Competent
64. City in Alaska
65. Trade
67. Lion feature
68. Bacchanal's cry
69. Scorch
72. Collection of facts

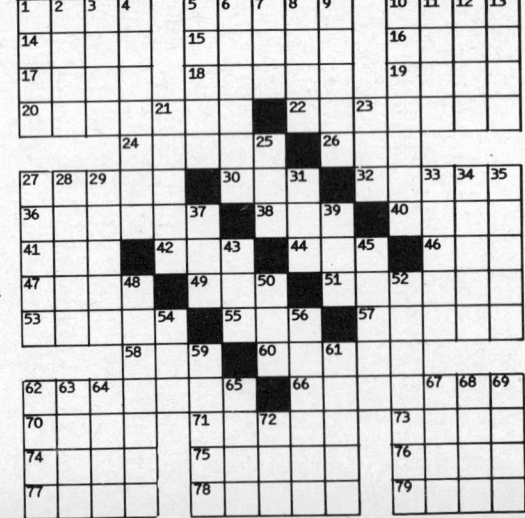

(Answers on page 195.)

Puzzle 3

ACROSS

1. Coffee: sl.
5. Yawns
10. —— facto
14. Wallet items
15. Acquiesce
16. Brad, e.g.
17. Holy women: abbr.
18. French river
19. Bell sound
20. Continued story
22. Among: poetic
23. Concept
24. Greek portico
26. Fitzgerald
28. Asserts
32. Mediterranean sea
36. Greek god
37. Unlocks
39. —— Grande
40. Ethiopian title
41. Odd
43. Actor —— Byrnes
44. Baseball's Mel
45. River of England
46. Snick and ——
47. Tenant
49. Frontiersmen
52. Oriental nurse
54. Out of the ordinary
55. Soapstone
58. Distress signal
60. Connected
64. Winglike
65. Join together
67. Challenge
68. Tennis word
69. Ex-Yankee Maris
70. Otherwise
71. Go first
72. Sea eagles
73. Critic Rex

DOWN

1. Chinese idol
2. Poker stake
3. Swerve
4. Helps
5. Liquid measure
6. In the past
7. —— and proper
8. Uncanny
9. Young plant
10. Sioux or Kiowa
11. Settled a bill
12. Without: Latin
13. Girl's name
21. Consumed
25. Idolize
27. Misplace
28. Actress Lawrence
29. Speechify
30. Cozy places
31. Bridges
33. Girl of song
34. —— and abettor
35. Small lumps
38. Come in
41. Stalk
42. "—— Island"
46. Thin
48. Hallowed
50. Old German coins
51. Three: pref.
53. Esteem
55. Lofty
56. Lilylike plant
57. Volcanic matter
59. Affix one's name
61. Cabbage variety
62. Irish-Gaelic
63. Exploit
66. Golfer's device

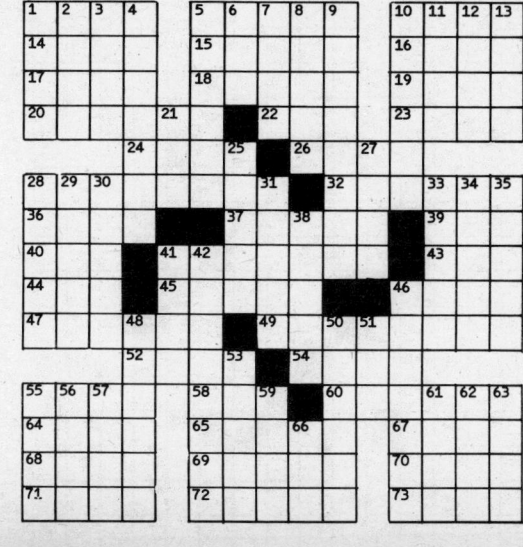

(Answers on page 196.)

Puzzle 4

ACROSS

1. Cleanser
5. God of War
9. La Scala feature
14. Unconstraint
15. Wander
16. Punitive
17. Fascinated
19. Commonplace
20. Identical
21. Pester
23. —— of March
24. Makes wrathful
27. Western alliance
29. Withdraws
32. Heckle
36. "Ben ——"
37. Poetry muse
39. New York county
40. Tentmaker-poet
42. Fixed look
44. Stopper
45. Strikes an attitude
47. Glossy; smooth
49. River in Scotland
50. Builds
52. Sincere
54. Sups
56. Tinted
57. Biblical trio
60. Still
62. Ireland
65. Active
67. Enrolls
71. Rural byways
72. Futile
73. Nebraska Indian
74. Exchange
75. Work units
76. Remainder

DOWN

1. One of seven
2. Cereal grain
3. Fictional dog
4. Allow
5. Circle part
6. Twaddle: sl.
7. Level
8. French city
9. Choose
10. Intermittent
11. City in Oklahoma
12. Classify
13. Pub drinks
18. Eagle's nest
22. Chew the fat
25. Blunders
26. Shows to a chair
28. Tit for ——
29. Hearsay
30. Clean a blackboard
31. Tasteless
33. Wares
34. Wading bird
35. Do a lawn job
36. Anticipation
38. Mountain nymph
41. Acquired
43. Weird
46. Depot: abbr.
48. Leg joints
51. Farm feature
53. Newspaper man
55. Wait on
57. Beer ingredient
58. Winged
59. Lollobrigida
61. Sign of sorrow
63. Network
64. Cupid
66. Compass point
68. Job: sl.
69. Office holders
70. Place

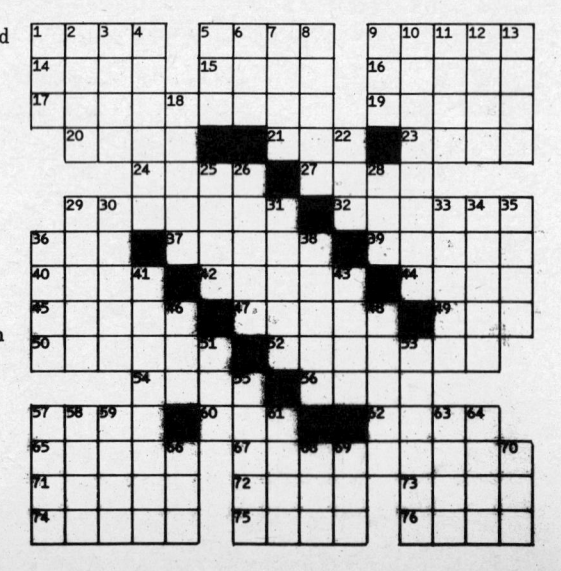

(Answers on page 197.)

ANSWERS

Lesson 1

1. needle-shaped   2. too much acid in the blood   3. to embitter or irritate   4. to make slightly acid   5. have a high acid content, sour tasting   6. c   7. b   8. a   9. b

Lesson 2

1. action; place where business is done   2. list of things to be done   3. opponent   4. agility   5. aggravate   6. agitated   7. agonized   8. aggrandized

Lesson 3

1. the excuse that one was elsewhere when an event took place   2. symbolic representation of truths, ideals, or generalizations   3. one's own, cannot be taken away   4. to turn away, transfer to another   5. form of reproduction by cross-fertilization   6. b   7. d   8. c   9. a

Lesson 4

1. annual commemoration of an event   2. happening every three years   3. 200th anniversary, occurring every 200 years   4. spread over a year   5. d   6. e   7. f   8. b   9. c   10. a

Lesson 5

1. love of man, generosity   2. giving human characteristics to non-human things   3. belief in man as center of all things   4. the study of the origins and development of mankind   5. device for measuring parts of the human body   6. the science of man and man's development   7. the study of man's language, institutions, physical character, and customs   8. one who studies the science of man's origins and development

Lesson 6

1. religious leader   2. high-ranking bishop   3. one who designs buildings   4. model, prototype   5. universal rule, a government by all   6. d   7. a   8. e   9. b   10. c

Lesson 7

1. study of stars and their effect on human destiny   2. device to observe position of the stars   3. the mapping out of the heavenly bodies   4. scientist who studies heavenly phenomena   5. starlike object in space   6. astrophysics   7. astronaut   8. astrocyte   9. asterisk

Lesson 8

1. gathering place for audience   2. relating to sound or reproduction of sound   3. a critical hearing   4. a tape recording of sound   5. related to use of hearing and sight   6. inaudible   7. audit   8. audition   9. auditory   10. audiophile

Answers

Lesson 9

1. scientist who studies life   2. written account of another's life   3. diagnostic study of living tissue   4. production of living organisms from other living organisms   5. an account of one's life, written by oneself   6. area consisting of specific vegetation and climate   7. living matter   8. effects of climate on life   9. medical field dealing with relationship of body chemistry to function   10. that part of earth's crust, water, and air where life can exist

Lesson 10

1. giving off heat   2. heat producing   3. instrument to measure quantities of heat   4. the measurement of heat   5. impregnating steel with aluminum by using heat   6. a large boiler

Lesson 11

1. device to receive and hold electrical charge   2. able to receive ideas   3. responsive, little resistance to stimuli   4. to receive   5. to take by fraud   6. a   7. b   8. b   9. b

Lesson 12

1. to surrender   2. each person, every head   3. a heading of a chapter of a book   4. profits from sale of property or stock   5. device to change key of guitar, banjo, etc., that is attached to neck and head of instrument   6. e   7. c   8. a   9. b   10. d

Lesson 13

1. warm, heartfelt   2. to inspire with courage   3. be in agreement   4. not agreeable, unharmonious   5. electronic device to record the action of the heart   6. agreement   7. shaped like a heart

Lesson 14

1. to charge a person with wrongdoing   2. to remove the blame, to make apology for   3. a reason for an event or action   4. without motive   5. the relation of cause and effect   6. a theory stating every event is a result of an adequate motive

Lesson 15

1. to mediate   2. a previous event   3. death   4. to go beyond the limits   5. a forward action   6. b   7. c   8. c   9. d   10. c

Lesson 16

1. pertaining to colors, often in music shading   2. protoplasm containing pigment   3. easily stainable with dyes   4. sensitive to all visible colors   5. having one color   6. visual defect where the eye fails to perceive color   7. involving only two colors

Lesson 17

1. a sequential order of events   2. device that shows if two related machines are operating at the same time   3. device to transmit time signals electronically   4. an historian   5. instrument that measures brief time intervals   6. d   7. e   8. b   9. a   10. c

Answers

Lesson 18

1. civilian   2. civility   3. uncivil   4. civil war
5. civilize

Lesson 19

1. to make a formal speech   2. to disown, deny   3. a crying out   4. not called for   5. one who makes a claim   6. one who seizes another's property   7. an insurance adjuster

Lesson 20

1. shut away   2. to close the way to   3. to close, bring to an end   4. to prevent an occurrence   5. one who lives in seclusion, one shut away   6. excluding others   7. a separate section of a piece of writing

Lesson 21

1. to perceive   2. to predict the future from present signs and indications   3. c   4. d   5. b   6. b

Lesson 22

1. physical body   2. to bring persons together into a legal entity   3. a legal association   4. large body   5. cell   6. a member of a corporation

Lesson 23

1. refined   2. impolite   3. a prostitute, associated with noblemen   4. wooing of woman by a man
5. court open to the sky

Lesson 24

1. having ability to originate   2. able to produce
3. anything created; animal or inanimate   4. to revive, bring into existence again   5. misbelieving
6. ability to be creative   8. one who creates; God

Lesson 25

1. acceptance as truth   2. deserving esteem
3. evidence of authority   4. business firm that investigates financial standing   5. not worthy of belief   6. d   7. c   8. c   9. a   10. d

Lesson 26

1. recurring in cycles   2. device for measuring arcs of a circle   3. books containing wide selection of information   4. one who travels by uni-, bi-, or tricycle   5. eels with circular mouths
6. mythological creature with a single, round eye in the middle of the forehead   7. a two-wheeled vehicle, propelled by pedals   8. a one-wheeled device, driven by pedals   9. resembling a circle   10. a device that measures the revolutions of a wheel

Lesson 27

1. hard tissue that makes up teeth   2. one who straightens teeth   3. resembling teeth   4. false teeth   5. the kind, number, and arrangement of the teeth of man and animals   6. having the shape of teeth   7. one who deals with tooth diseases

# Answers

Lesson 28

1. evil words   2. one who rules absolutely   3. charge with an offense   4. something that points out
5. argue   6. d   7. b   8. c   9. c   10. a

Lesson 29

1. bedroom window   2. lying asleep   3. motionless
4. causing sleep   5. a dormitory

Lesson 30

1. single-humped camel   2. airport   3. horse racing track   4. auto racing   5. warning symptom   6. a device used to measure speed   7. a chart used to record speed changes

Lesson 31

1. e   2. h   3. a   4. j   5. c   6. f   7. i   8. g
9. d   10. b

Lesson 32

1. inside the stomach   2. within the bone
3. instrument to examine inside of the body   4. a mineral within another mineral   5. nutritive matter within seed plant ovules   6. plant living within another plant   7. within the heart   8. inner layer of a fruit

Lesson 33

1. an ability   2. the act of making one fulfilled   3. an element of a situation; one who transacts business for another   4. easily done   5. dexterity   6. b   7. c
8. b   9. a   10. a

Lesson 34

1. an union based on agreement   2. one who has no faith   3. without trust, deceitful   4. an accomplice   5. in good faith   6. faith in oneself   7. a written oath   8. one to whom property or power is entrusted for another   9. engaged   10. group united for a common action

Lesson 35

1. one who receives advantages   2. able to make or do things well   3. making objects resemble people   4. faulty, not made well   5. to make a false impression of one's self   6. making poems   7. adequate, enough made   8. the act of making one known   9. a result, make happen   10. made without flaws; exactly made

Lesson 36

1. c   2. e   3. a   4. h   5. g   6. b   7. d   8. f

Lesson 37

1. ornamental work with fine threadlike wire   2. a reel for drawing silk from cocoons   3. threadlike   4. relating to thread   5. slender, threadlike worms   6. drawing of something in outline form

Lesson 38

1. the ending of something, especially the last section of a musical composition   2. a sum of money paid as penalty   3. topmost ornament on furniture or lamp   4. having limits or an end   5. without ending or limits   6. to set a limit   7. the end of a century (French)   8. a contestant in the finals of a competition

Answers

Lesson 39

1. one who takes care of things   2. to attach   3. to hold motionless   4. substance used to make permanent, like glue   5. being attached   6. in a difficult position   7. repaired   8. furniture, in a permanent place

Lesson 40

1. to bend at the knee in prayer   2. a muscle that helps bend a limb   3. easily bent, tractable   4. a printing process using rubber plates   5. c   6. a   7. f   8. e   9. d   10. b

Lesson 41

1. a flowing in   2. capable of flowing, like speech   3. extra, more flowing in   4. meeting place of rivers   5. a disagreeable vapor   6. b   7. c   8. b   9. a   10. a

Lesson 42

1. an agent or material used in fumigating   2. volcanic hole   3. a place for smoking   4. smokelike   5. person who fumigates   6. c   7. b   8. a   9. e   10. d

Lesson 43

1. good birth and family   2. man of good birth   3. people of rank   4. a biological category system for classification of life forms   5. favorable to growth   6. d   7. a   8. b   9. e   10. c

Lesson 44

1. the process of growing or sprouting   2. life repellant   3. possessing ability to germinate   4. having germs   5. relevant and appropriate   6. a   7. c   8. e   9. b   10. d

Lesson 45

1. communicate by means of motions   2. full of motion   3. to overcrowd   4. pregnant   5. having to do with bodily functions   6. b   7. e   8. a   9. c   10. d

Lesson 46

1. to determine, seek knowledge of   2. having no knowledge of   3. a forecast based on knowledge   4. understanding   5. to know from a previous time   6. d   7. c   8. b   9. a   10. e

Lesson 47

1. to go or walk forward   2. promote to a higher step   3. to go beyond   4. to move or walk against in an attack   5. step back, retreat   6. b   7. d   8. c   9. a   10. e

Lesson 48

1. reproduction of writing   2. apparatus for making reproductions of samples of writing   3. correct writing   4. instrument for reproducing recorded sound   5. study of earth's surface as written on maps   6. a   7. e   8. b   9. c   10. d

Answers

Lesson 49

1. extra money received in gratitude   2. thanklessness
3. to give pleasure   4. thankful   5. state of being grateful   6. e   7. d   8. b   9. c   10. a

Lesson 50

1. obeying the law of gravity   2. weight
3. measurement of weight   4. tending to gravitate
5. hypothetical particle   6. b   7. a   8. d   9. c
10. e

Lesson 51

1. herd or crowd-like   2. to gather into a group
3. not part of the group, standing out from the crowd
4. to set apart from the group   5. having to do with the forming of a crowd   6. b   7. d   8. a   9. e
10. c

Lesson 52

1. place of living   2. to make accustomed to
3. resident   4. to live together   5. having to do with habit   6. b   7. d   8. a   9. c   10. e

Lesson 53

1. instrument using the sun's rays for sending messages   2. message transmitted by heliograph
3. having a relation to the center of the sun   4. plant that thrives in sunlight   5. instrument used to observe the sun   6. e   7. d   8. c   9. b   10. a

Lesson 54

1. having to do with blood   2. instrument designed to temporarily stop bleeding   3. gorged with blood   4. a blood cell   5. the element in blood giving it its red color   6. d   7. c   8. e   9. a   10. b

Lesson 55

1. fear of water   2. an airplane capable of landing on water   3. movement by means of forcing water through a propeller   4. an instrument used to see through or into water   5. free from water   6. b   7. a   8. d   9. c   10. e

Lesson 56

1. exhibiting fear of sleep   2. the practice of hypnosis   3. relating to sleep   4. being able to be hypnotized   5. having to do with sleep or hypnosis   6. e   7. b   8. a   9. d   10. c

Lesson 57

1. something which can be known   2. the ability to think or know   3. the incapability to think or know   4. most intelligent group, intellectual elite   5. a person devoted to knowledge-seeking   6. c   7. e   8. a   9. d   10. b

Lesson 58

1. to throw out   2. to throw (insert) in   3. to surmise   4. a throwing in a forward direction   5. to throw back, refuse to accept   6. e   7. a   8. d   9. b   10. c

Answers

Lesson 59

1. joined with 2. having a tendency to join 3. direct by order 4. to separate 5. a joining or coming together 6. a 7. c 8. b 9. e 10. d

Lesson 60

1. having to do with the fair administration of justice 2. one having authority to decree judgment 3. a decision 4. biased 5. having the capability of being judged 6. a 7. e 8. d 9. b 10. c

Lesson 61

1. the science of law 2. a false swearing instead of truthful testimony 3. the authority to interpret and administer the law 4. to solemnly renounce 5. to implore solemnly or earnestly 6. e 7. a 8. c 9. b 10. d

Lesson 62

1. to exert one's body with effort 2. worked at ridiculous length 3. replacing or decreasing human labor 4. a person who labors 5. a person who favors the interests of labor 6. performed with labor 7. involving much effort or toil

Lesson 63

1. ceremony where hands are washed 2. flood of water 3. wash away 4. state of being diluted 5. to wash 6. b 7. e 8. c 9. a 10. d

Lesson 64

1. legal, law-abiding   2. lawmaker   3. the giver of a legacy   4. to give a legacy   5. to put a law into enactment   6. d   7. a   8. c   9. e   10. b

Lesson 65

1. the concept of representing something by using words   2. not able to read   3. "to the letter," exactly   4. the recurrence of the same letter sound   5. to spell in the letters of another alphabet   6. e   7. c   8. a   9. b   10. d

Lesson 66

1. the concept of freedom   2. the killing of freedom   3. to make free   4. to add freedoms   5. not liberal, bigoted   6. b   7. d   8. e   9. a   10. c

Lesson 67

1. the act of giving out permits or licenses
2. authorized, allowed   3. the giving out of licenses
4. the concept of being illegal   5. self-given permission to act in disregard of rules   6. c   7. b   8. e   9. a   10. d

Lesson 68

1. site, scene   2. to remove from proper place
3. self-propelled engine   4. place   5. the ability to move from one place to another   6. a   7. d   8. e   9. c   10. b

Answers

Lesson 69

1. narrated travel film   2. a person skilled in logic   3. dramatic soliloquy   4. the military art of supply and personnel transport   5. the worship of logic   6. b   7. c   8. a   9. e   10. d

Lesson 70

1. dramatic monologue   2. a person able to "throw" his voice, making it appear to come from another source   3. the concept of speaking comfortably and with ease   4. the state of being very talkative   5. articulate   6. e   7. b   8. a   9. c   10. d

Lesson 71

1. make clear, bring into the light   2. a misleading vision   3. shining   4. student   5. a unit of measure for light   6. d   7. a   8. e   9. b   10. c

Lesson 72

1. great in deed or place   2. a shrub with large (great) flowers   3. greatness   4. make larger or greater   5. a document granting rights (from the English magna charta in 1215)   6. a   7. d   8. e   9. c   10. b

Lesson 73

1. obvious   2. operate by hand   3. move by manipulation   4. handbook   5. a place where products are produced by hand   6. b   7. d   8. a   9. c   10. e

Lesson 74

1. a soldier serving on shipboard   2. a panorama consisting of, for the most part, the sea   3. a fabled sea creature—half-woman, half-fish   4. lake or pool   5. wetland or swamp   6. d   7. a   8. b   9. c   10. e

Lesson 75

1. something within which something else develops   2. a school from which one has graduated   3. tracing of lineage through the mother   4. state of wedlock   5. the condition of being a mother   6. d   7. b   8. a   9. c   10. e

Lesson 76

1. of moderate quality   2. being next in line   3. being in the middle   4. having to do with the Middle Ages   5. d   6. e   7. a   8. c   9. b

Lesson 77

1. a unit of measure of radio frequency equaling one million cycles per second   2. a unit of measure of explosive force equaling the explosive force of one million tons of dynamite   3. large urban unit   4. large-footed   5. prehistoric stone monument   6. a   7. e   8. d   9. c   10. b

Lesson 78

1. to call to mind, serve as a memorial   2. things worthy of remembering   3. record of personal experiences   4. written reminder   5. abbreviation of memorandum   6. b   7. c   8. e   9. a   10. d

Answers

Lesson 79

1. a device for measuring atmospheric pressure
2. balanced proportions
3. a branch of mathematics dealing with measurements of solids, surfaces, lines, and angles
4. a device used to measure altitude
5. d   6. b   7. a   8. c

Lesson 80

1. a unit of measure of length equaling one thousandth of a millimeter
2. a little world
3. a reduction of size of photographic display
4. having to do with microbes
5. a (copy of printed material or a photograph) which is reduced in size
6. e   7. c   8. d   9. b   10. a

Lesson 81

1. the belief of passing, at death, from one body to another
2. having to do with immigration
3. tending to emigrate
4. b   5. d   6. e   7. a   8. c

Lesson 82

1. the carrying out of some task or mission
2. to send away
3. to send money in payment of a bill; to postpone
4. to allow
5. to send from one person or place to another person or place
6. c   7. a   8. d   9. b   10. e

Lesson 83

1. something that causes movement 2. a cause or need of a person (what moves them to do something) 3. to move to a higher rank 4. to move to a lower rank 5. the act of moving from one place to another 6. b 7. c 8. e 9. d 10. a

Lesson 84

1. a display 2. showing opposition 3. having to do with a demonstration 4. opposition 5. abnormally developed being 6. d 7. a 8. b 9. c 10. e

Lesson 85

1. a place where corpses are kept until burial 2. undertaker 3. the subjection of one to humiliation 4. not subject to death 5. deathlike 6. b 7. e 8. c 9. d 10. a

Lesson 86

1. crowdlike 2. manifold 3. many feet 4. giving birth to more than one 5. a person possessing more than two million dollars 6. a 7. d 8. b 9. c 10. e

Lesson 87

1. having to do with nature or something native to an area 2. a favoring of the native born 3. inborn 4. coming into being 5. place of origin 6. c 7. d 8. b 9. e 10. a

Answers

Lesson 88

1. a physician who treats diseases of the nervous system   2. originating in nervous tissue   3. a functional nervous disorder   4. like a nerve or like tissue   5. inflammation of a nerve   6. a   7. d   8. c   9. b   10. e

Lesson 89

1. to accuse   2. to refuse by declaration   3. act of announcing   4. papal representative working as envoy with a country's government   5. a person who makes public announcements   6. e   7. d   8. b   9. c   10. a

Lesson 90

1. renew   2. a star that is suddenly very bright   3. a drug that deadens nerves   4. introduction of something new   5. the period of being a beginner   6. b   7. c   8. a   9. d   10. e

Lesson 91

1. to count, to list   2. plentiful, many   3. denoting a number   4. having to do with counting   5. having no numbers   6. d   7. b   8. e   9. c   10. a

Lesson 92

1. a musical work   2. one who is operated on   3. the act of doing work   4. having to do with the act of work   5. petty or busy work   6. b   7. c   8. a   9. e   10. d

Lesson 93

1. having to do with bone   2. a large fish hawk nicknamed *breakbones*   3. small bone   4. bony   5. cemetery   6. c   7. b   8. e   9. d   10. a

Lesson 94

1. the support of a patron   2. to treat condescendingly; to act as a customer   3. founder; father figure   4. something inherited from one's father   5. the killing of one's father   6. c   7. d   8. a   9. b   10. e

Lesson 95

1. triangular decoration over a door or window   2. the support base, or foot of something   3. to hinder or block progress   4. foot doctor   5. possessing three feet   6. a   7. e   8. d   9. b   10. c

Lesson 96

1. to motivate; to drive onward   2. to drive away   3. to throw out   4. regular throbbing caused in the arteries by heart contractions; beat   5. actions suddenly or momentarily   6. b   7. a   8. d   9. e   10. c

Lesson 97

1. something attached to a principal or main body   2. a brief summary of a larger work   3. a fixed sum of money paid at regular intervals   4. d   5. a   6. e   7. b   8. c

Answers

Lesson 98

1. a charm kept to excite sexual love affairs   3. the fondness for women Greece   5. lover of all finer things   2. to have love   4. an admirer of   6. b   7. c   8. a   9. e   10. d

Lesson 99

1. giving a large image of a distant object   2. production of carbohydrates by plants utilizing light as a raw material   3. light-seeking, moving toward light   4. a nonmetallic element that displays a faint glow in moist air   5. a chemical salt with a base element of phosphorous   6. d   7. e   8. c   9. b   10. a

Lesson 100

1. writing which utilizes pictures instead of words   2. picture transmitted electronically   3. painter   4. make a picture of   5. picture-like quality   6. c   7. a   8. b   9. d   10. e

Lesson 101

1. a useless, but pleasing medication   2. not capable of being pleased   3. one that pleases   4. state of being calm   5. act of pleasing   6. e   7. b   8. c   9. d   10. a

Lesson 102

1. to make plural   2. the act of making more than one   3. the state of being plural   4. word having two or more syllables   5. having two or more names   6. e   7. c   8. b   9. d   10. a

Lesson 103

1. relating to the lungs   2. an affinity for lung tissues   3. c   4. d   5. a   6. e   7. b

Lesson 104

1. one who positions himself on your side   2. to place back to a later time   3. one who gives written evidence   4. to assume   5. a place where something is deposited   6. e   7. a   8. d   9. b   10. c

Lesson 105

1. to cut down the number of people   2. not liked by the people   3. genocide   4. basic ideas expressed by populist party   5. the number of people inhabiting a given area   6. c   7. e   8. b   9. a   10. d

Lesson 106

1. a gatherer and carrier of news   2. agree, accord, behave   3. divert, amuse   4. to carry goods to foreign countries for purpose of trade   5. to carry goods into your country from a foreign country for purpose of consumption   6. a   7. c   8. e   9. b   10. d

Lesson 107

1. to share out; divide   2. divided into similar sizes or amounts   3. not comparably divided   4. d   5. b   6. a   7. c   8. e

Answers

Lesson 108

1. amount of power   2. possessing authority or power   3. to own legally   4. capability of future power   5. to make powerful   6. a   7. e   8. d   9. b   10. c

Lesson 109

1. having to do with the earliest ages   2. a book for children (the first reading book)   3. first developed   4. firstborn rights of inheritance   5. powerful bishop   6. d   7. a   8. e   9. b   10. c

Lesson 110

1. perfectness, exactness   2. one applying standardized marks to a sentence   3. the process of punctuating   4. remorse   5. on time (on the dot)   6. b   7. a   8. c   9. e   10. d

Lesson 111

1. to count responsible for   2. a person standing in to act for another   3. to cut off   4. overall character as seen by others   5. the act of counting   6. c   7. e   8. a   9. b   10. d

Lesson 112

1. a clergyman   2. righteousness   3. a book of rules or directions   4. sum total, product of calculation   5. to make right   6. b   7. e   8. a   9. d   10. c

Lesson 113

1. able to laugh   2. laughing   3. causing scornful laughing   4. to mock   5. the ability to be able to laugh; possessing a sense of humor   6. b   7. d   8. e   9. c   10. a

Lesson 114

1. a moderate to strong red   2. enthusiasm   3. murderously   4. pale   5. bloody   6. a   7. b   8. d   9. e   10. d

Lesson 115

1. an instrument for seeing various designs made by changing bits of glass   2. a rapidly spinning wheel mounted on an axis   3. instrument for safely viewing the sun   4. providing a view on all sides   5. device for detecting radioactive substances   6. b   7. c   8. a   9. e   10. d

Lesson 116

1. an appointment for a lovers' meeting   2. to formally deliver   3. to mark or point out   4. to make a pattern or plan for something   5. to give up deliberately by a formal act (usually by signing a statement)   6. d   7. b   8. a   9. e   10. c

Lesson 117

1. lung disease caused by inhaling stone dust   2. containing silica   3. relating to silica or silicon   4. e   5. b   6. d   7. c   8. a

Answers

Lesson 118

1. to create the appearance of   2. the quality of appearing to be true   3. occurring at the same time   4. a likeness of an image   5. resemblance
6. d   7. e   8. b   9. a   10. c

Lesson 119

1. to receive means of sustaining life   2. being   3. position or rank in relation to others   4. to withstand opposition   5. to continue resolutely
6. d   7. b   8. a   9. c   10. e

Lesson 120

1. lover of wisdom   2. false reasoner   3. worldly-wise; artificial   4. science of ideas   5. having to do with wisdom   6. e   7. d   8. b   9. a   10. c

Lesson 121

1. the act of looking inward   2. an observation from a particular aspect   3. to look at from all angles; a considering from all points of view   4. ability to see shrewdly   5. to look into; to look at closely   6. b
7. d   8. e   9. c   10. a

Lesson 122

1. the state of being spherical   2. area surrounding the earth between earth's surface and stratosphere   3. a sphere of light; light which surrounds the sun's surface   4. earth's solid mass   5. the crust of the earth   6. b   7. c   8. e   9. a   10. d

Lesson 123

1. to act as a patron for; to answer for   2. answerable
3. written communications   4. one who answers
5. having to do with being a sponsor   6. a   7. d
8. e   9. c   10. b

Lesson 124

1. ruin; the action of destroying   2. something built on a base   3. teach; inform; to give directions to   4. to block the passage, action, or operation of   5. having to do with something built   6. e   7. d   8. a   9. c   10. b

Lesson 125

1. to take upon oneself without permission   2. to devour; to spend wastefully; to destroy (as by fire)
3. lavish showing   4. displaying audacity   5. the taking up again or assuming again   6. b   7. e   8. c   9. a   10. d

Lesson 126

1. a keen sense of what to do   2. perceptible, especially by sense of touch   3. an infection caused usually by touching   4. touching   5. intertwined   6. c
7. a   8. b   9. e   10. d

Lesson 127

1. receptacle for holding   2. to hold in   3. to achieve; reach   4. to hold in mind; receive as a guest   5. to gain   6. b   7. c   8. a   9. d   10. e

Answers

Lesson 128

1. science of mechanical skills   2. person holding an interest in a technical area   3. fireworks; a brilliant display   4. society run by technicians   5. the science of industrial arts   6. c   7. d   8. e   9. a   10. b

Lesson 129

1. done or spoken without preparation   2. rate of speed in music   3. for a limited time   4. to give in for a short time to current opinion   5. b   6. a   7. c   8. d   9. e

Lesson 130

1. expand   2. to direct   3. the act of straining or stretching   4. meaning, goal, purpose   5. apparent; professed   6. c   7. a   8. e   9. b   10. d

Lesson 131

1. to bear witness   2. tribute; a statement upholding either a person's character or the quality of something   3. fight, argument, struggle   4. to hate   5. the process of making a will   6. d   7. e   8. a   9. c   10. b

Lesson 132

1. belief in one god   2. government by divine guidance   3. the belief that equates god with all forces and laws of the universe   4. belief which denies the existence of god   5. deification   6. e   7. b   8. d   9. a   10. c

Lesson 133

1. possessing qualities which draw someone or something towards oneself   2. to remove, separate   3. to withdraw   4. to draw out   5. c   6. d   7. b   8. e   9. a

Lesson 134

1. the act of dividing among many   2. a gift given to help or aid   3. explanation of cause or origin   4. to divide again among many   5. revenge, payback   6. b   7. e   8. a   9. d   10. c

Lesson 135

1. payment for instruction   2. having to do with a tutor   3. knowledge obtained by insight   4. power of intuitive thought   5. one who is a believer in intuition   6. e   7. a   8. d   9. c   10. b

Lesson 136

1. having the form or manner of one   2. one-wheeled vehicle   3. legendary, one-horned, horse-like animal   4. having a single legislative house   5. having a single cell   6. c   7. e   8. a   9. b   10. d

Lesson 137

1. holiday from work   2. a purgative; agent causing an emptying   3. state of being empty   4. to empty; make void   5. a void   6. e   7. b   8. d   9. a   10. c

Answers

Lesson 138

1. widespread   2. brave, valorous   3. equal in value   4. a farewell   5. d   6. a   7. e   8. c   9. b

Lesson 139

1. to occur, fall or come between points of time   2. to occur as something additional   3. an undertaking involving chance or risk   4. arrival   5. to halt or defeat an opponent by using strategy   6. c   7. a   8. b   9. e   10. d

Lesson 140

1. truly   2. the appearance of truth   3. to declare positively   4. decision; judgment   5. truly; certainly   6. b   7. e   8. a   9. d   10. c

Lesson 141

1. the overthrowing; the corruption   2. incapable of being reversed   3. top, summit, zenith   4. to change into a different form   5. c   6. d   7. a   8. e   9. b

Lesson 142

1. outer clothing   2. having to do with clothing   3. to buy something for future profit; to furnish with authority   4. e   5. a   6. d   7. c   8. b

Lesson 143

1. in the manner of a substitute   2. a change in luck or fortune   3. having a change in fortune   4. bombarded with changes of fortune (usually for the worse)   5. delegated   6. d   7. a   8. e   9. b   10. c

Lesson 144

1. triumph; winning   2. act of proving a person guilty   3. act of throwing a person out   4. win over   5. undefeatable   6. d   7. e   8. a   9. c   10. b

Lesson 145

1. the act or power of seeing   2. to give advice   3. person given to dreaming or imagining   4. clear to the vision or understanding   5. envious; injurious   6. e   7. b   8. d   9. a   10. c

Lesson 146

1. capacity to live   2. full of life and vigor   3. the action required to maintain life   4. the act of bringing something back to life   5. lively in temper or conduct   6. c   7. a   8. b   9. e   10. d

Lesson 147

1. to grant or give by favor or condescension   2. clamorous; given to loud outcries   3. one who pleads in behalf of another   4. a word composed of various sounds without regard to its meaning   5. to call together to a meeting   6. b   7. a   8. d   9. c

Answers

Lesson 148

1. the study of volcanoes and volcanic eruptions
2. power of a volcano   3. the chemical procedure required to produce a rubberlike substance   4. d
5. b   6. a   7. e   8. c

Puzzle 1

S	E	A	L		B	A	R	B		R	O	B	E	S
C	A	G	E		A	L	E	E		E	V	A	D	E
A	G	I	O		H	O	A	R		F	A	I	N	T
R	E	L			E	L	E	M	I		L	A	S	
E	R	E	C	T	S		T	A	N	G				
			O	I	L	E	R		D	E	L	E	T	E
C	H	A	N	N	E	L	E	D		D	A	L	E	S
H	U	N	T		W	A	F	E	R		S	L	A	P
A	L	T	E	R		N	E	C	E	S	S	A	R	Y
P	A	S	S	E	S		R	A	N	E	E			
			T	A	I	L		T	E	S	T	E	D	
E	S	T		C	R	E	E	K			A	V	A	
A	W	A	S	H		G	R	I	P		O	N	E	R
R	A	R	E	E		A	N	T	A		P	I	N	E
S	T	E	W	S		L	E	E	R		T	A	T	S

Puzzle 2

T	A	M	E		S	T	A	L	E		D	R	A	M
I	B	E	X		A	A	R	O	N		R	I	L	E
F	I	A	T		D	I	E	T	S		I	T	E	R
F	E	D	E	R	A	L		S	U	R	F	A	C	E
			N	O	T	E	S		E	A	T			
C	R	E	D	O		D	U	E		M	E	D	A	L
R	O	A	S	T	S		M	O	B		D	O	L	E
E	G	G		S	A	G		N	I	P		P	I	G
S	E	L	L		W	I	T		G	E	N	E	V	A
T	R	E	A	D		N	U	T		E	A	S	E	L
			R	E	L		B	U	R	N	T			
T	A	N	G	L	E	S		R	E	S	U	M	E	S
E	B	O	E		A	W	A	R	E		R	A	V	E
A	L	M	S		P	A	N	E	L		A	N	O	A
M	E	E	T		S	P	A	T	S		L	E	E	R

Puzzle 3

```
J A V A . G A P E S . I P S O
O N E S . A G R E E . N A I L
S T E S . L O I R E . D I N G
S E R I A L . M I D . I D E A
. . . S T O A . E L L A . . .
C O N T E N D S . I O N I A N
A R E S . . O P E N S . R I O
R A S . S T R A N G E . E D D
O T T . T R E N T . . S N E E
L E S S E E . S E T T L E R S
. . . A M A H . R A R E . . .
T A L C . S O S . L I N K E D
A L A R . U N I T E . D A R E
L O V E . R O G E R . E L S E
L E A D . E R N E S . R E E D
```

Puzzle 4

```
S O A P . A R E S . O P E R A
E A S E . R O V E . P E N A L
A T T R A C T E D . T R I T E
. S A M E . N A G . I D E S
. . I R E S . N A T O . . .
. R E T I R E S . B A D G E R
H U R . E R A T O . T I O G A
O M A R . S T A R E . C O R K
P O S E S . S L E E K . D E E
E R E C T S . E A R N E S T .
. . . E A T S . D Y E D . .
M A G I . Y E T . E I R E .
A L I V E . R E G I S T E R S
L A N E S . V A I N . O T O E
T R A D E . E R G S . R E S T
```